PRAISE FOR
RON STALLWORTH'S STORY

WINNER OF THE CANNES FILM FESTIVAL GRAND PRIX

"I was just blown away. I couldn't believe I had never heard about it. It's one of these pieces of reality that almost plays like social satire. I was immediately obsessed with this story."
—Jordan Peele in *The Hollywood Reporter*

"A direct, furious protest against the Trump era."
—*The New York Times*

"The astonishing true story of one of the riskiest undercover investigations in American history—an improbable early-'70s case in which black police detective Ron Stallworth applied for and was ultimately granted membership in the Ku Klux Klan . . . A compelling black empowerment story."
—*Variety*

"Stallworth's story is so wild you can barely believe it—but certainly not wilder than the virulent resurgence of white supremacy in this country, so extreme it goes beyond the reach of satire."
—*Time* magazine

BLACK KLANSMAN

RACE, HATE, AND THE UNDERCOVER INVESTIGATION OF A LIFETIME

RON STALLWORTH

FLATIRON
BOOKS
NEW YORK

BLACK KLANSMAN. Copyright © 2014 by Ron Stallworth. All rights reserved. Printed in the United States of America. For information, address Flatiron Books, 175 Fifth Avenue, New York, N.Y. 10010.

www.flatironbooks.com

Photograph of civil rights activist Ralph Abernathy at a rally (pg. 8 of photo insert) by © Flip Schulke/CORBIS/Corbis via Getty Images.

All other photographs are courtesy of the author.

Designed by Steven Seighman

The Library of Congress has cataloged the hardcover edition as follows:

Names: Stallworth, Ron.
Title: Black Klansman : race, hate, and the undercover investigation of a
    lifetime / Ron Stallworth.
Description: New York : Flatiron Books, [2018]
Identifiers: LCCN 2018003659| ISBN 9781250299048 (hardcover) |
    ISBN 9781250299031 (ebook)
Subjects: LCSH: Stallworth, Ron. | Ku Klux Klan (1915–) | White supremacy
    movements—United States. | Hate crimes—United States. | Undercover
    operations—United States. | African American police. | United
    States—Race relations.
Classification: LCC HS2330.K63 S727 2018 | DDC 322.4/209788—dc23
LC record available at https://lccn.loc.gov/2018003659

ISBN 978-1-250-29905-5 (trade paperback)

Our books may be purchased in bulk for promotional, educational, or business use. Please contact your local bookseller or the Macmillan Corporate and Premium Sales Department at 1-800-221-7945, extension 5442, or by email at MacmillanSpecialMarkets@macmillan.com.

Originally published in 2014 under the same title by Police and Fire Publishing

First Flatiron Books Paperback Edition: July 2018

10 9 8 7 6 5 4 3 2 1

*For my wife, Patsy Terrazas-Stallworth,
and Mr. Elroy Bode*

CONTENTS

AUTHOR'S NOTE

If one black man, aided by a bevy of good, decent, dedicated, open-, and liberal-minded whites and Jews can succeed in prevailing over a group of white racists by making them look like the ignorant fools they truly are, then imagine what a nation of like-minded individuals can accomplish. Everything that follows was accomplished despite, and in spite of, the supremacists' claim in some cases to being highly educated, having more intelligence, and being far superior in every way to blacks and Jews, and anyone else they deemed inferior. My investigation of the KKK convinced me that sooner rather than later we *would*, in fact, *overcome* those who tried to define minorities by their own personal failings of racial, ethnic bias, bigotry, religious preference, and the false belief that people of color and others who did not fit their definition of "pure Aryan white" were not deserving of respect, much less of being classified as "people."

Each time a man stands up for an ideal, or acts to improve the lot of others, or strikes out against injustice, he sends forth a tiny ripple of hope.

—Robert Kennedy

The most common way people give up their power is by thinking they don't have any.

—Alice Walker

BLACK
KLANSMAN

1

A CALL FROM THE KLAN

All of this began in October 1978. As an Intelligence Unit detective for the Colorado Springs Police Department, the first black detective in the history of the department, I might add, one of my duties was to scan the two daily newspapers for any reports of information concerning any hint of subversive activity that might have an impact on the welfare and safety of Colorado Springs. It's surprising what some people will put in the paper: prostitution, obvious money schemes, that sort of thing mostly, but every once in a while there's something that really stands out. As I looked over the classified ads, one in particular caught my eye. It read:

> Ku Klux Klan
> For Information Contact
> P.O. Box 4771
> Security, Colorado
> 80230

Now there was something unusual.

The town of Security was a suburban housing development area located southeast of Colorado Springs near two main military bases: Fort Carson and NORAD (North American Aerospace Defense Command). The community was predominantly military, and there had been no known Klan activity in these parts.

So, I answered the ad.

I wrote a brief note to the P.O. box explaining that I was a white man interested in obtaining information regarding membership in the KKK and furthering the cause of the white race. I wrote that I was concerned with "niggers taking over things," and that I wanted to change that. I signed my real name, Ron Stallworth, gave the undercover phone number, which was an unlisted, untraceable line, and used the undercover address, also untraceable. I placed my note in an envelope and dropped it in the mailbox.

Why did I sign my real name to the note, which would go on to launch one of the most fascinating, and unique, investigations of my career? Like all of our undercover investigators, I maintained two separate undercover identities with the appropriate support identification, driver's licenses, credit cards, etc. So why did I have this lapse in judgment and make such a foolish mistake?

The simple answer is I was not thinking of a future investigation when I mailed the note. I was seeking a reply, expecting it would be in the form of literature such as a pamphlet or brochure of some kind. All in all I did not believe my efforts would have any traction beyond a few mundane auto-mailed responses. I believed this blatant placement of such an inflammatory racist ad was nothing more than a feeble attempt at a prank, and by answering it I would see how far the prank would play itself out.

Two weeks later, on November 1, 1978, the undercover phone line rang. I picked it up, and a voice said, "May I speak to Ron Stallworth?"

"This is he," I said.

"Hi. My name is Ken O'dell. I'm the local organizer of the Colorado Springs chapter of the KKK. I received your note in the mail."

Oh hell, where do I go from here? I thought.

"Okay," I said, stalling for time as I grabbed a pen and legal pad.

"I read what you wrote, and I'm wondering why you would like to join our cause?"

Why do I want to join the Klan? A question I truly thought I never would have been asked, and I felt like saying, "Well, I want to get as much information as possible from you, Ken, so I can destroy the Klan and everything it stands for." But I didn't say that. Instead I took a deep breath and thought about what someone wanting to join the Klan would actually say.

I knew from being called a nigger many times in my life, from small confrontations in everyday life that escalated to an ugly rhetoric, to being on the job when I was giving someone a ticket or making an arrest, that when a white person would say that to me, the whole dynamic would change. By saying "nigger" he'd let me know he thought he was inherently better than me. That word was a way of claiming some false power. That is the language of hate, and now, having to pretend to be a white supremacist, I knew to use that language in reverse.

"Well, I hate niggers, Jews, Mexicans, spics, chinks, and

anyone else that does not have pure white Aryan blood in their veins," I said, and with those words I knew my undercover investigation had begun.

I continued, "My sister was recently involved with a nigger and every time I think about him putting his filthy black hands on her pure white body I get disgusted and sick to my stomach. I want to join the Klan so I can stop future abuse of the white race."

Ken sure warmed up at that point, his voice easing into something sweet and friendly. He identified himself as a Fort Carson soldier who lived in Security with his wife.

"And what exactly does the Klan plan on doing?" I asked, pen at the ready.

"We have a lot of plans. With the Christmas holiday approaching we're planning a 'White Christmas' for needy white families. No niggers need apply," Ken said.

They were seeking monetary donations through the P.O. box, and The Organization, as he referred to it, not the Klan, maintained a bank account under the name of "White People, Org" at a bank in Security.

"We're also planning four cross burnings. To announce our presence. We don't know exactly when yet, but that's what we want to do." My pen paused over my notes as I heard this. Four burnings here in Colorado Springs? Terrorism, plain and simple.

Ken went on to explain that membership in The Organization would cost ten dollars for the remainder of the year, thirty dollars for the next year, and I would have to buy my own hood and robe.

"When can you meet?" he asked.

Shit, I thought, *how do I meet this guy?* "Ahh, I can't for a week," I said.

"Well then, how about next Thursday night? The Kwik Inn, do you know it?"

"Yes," I replied.

"Seven o'clock. There'll be a tall, skinny, hippie-looking white guy with a Fu Manchu mustache, smoking a cigar outside. He'll meet you, then if it all looks okay, he'll take you to me," said Ken.

"Okay," I said, scribbling furiously in my pad.

"How will we recognize you?" Ken asked.

The same question I had been asking myself since I picked up the phone. How would I, a black cop, go undercover with white supremacists? I immediately thought of Chuck, an undercover narcotics cop I work with who was about my height and build.

"I'm about five foot nine, a hundred eighty pounds. I have dark hair and a beard," I said.

"Okay then. Nice talking to you, Ron. You're just the kind of person we're looking for. Looking forward to meeting you." And with that, the line went dead.

I took a deep breath and thought, *What the fuck am I going to do now?*

2

JACKIE ROBINSON
AND BLACK PANTHERS

Well, what I had to do was start an undercover investigation into the Klan and their plans to grow in my town. I had been working as an undercover investigator for four years, and had headed up many cases, but this one was going to be different, to say the least.

I hadn't grown up wanting to be a cop. In fact, I always wanted to be a high school PE teacher, and the way to put myself through college was to become a cadet for the Colorado Springs Police Department.

I was hired by the city of Colorado Springs on November 13, 1972, as a police cadet at nineteen years old. The cadet program was designed for high school graduates between the ages of seventeen and nineteen who desired a career in law enforcement. Applicants underwent the same battery of tests as regular police candidates and were required to pass them with the same scores because they were, in essence, officers-in-training. Once accepted into the program, the young applicants were paid a beginning salary of $5.25 per hour, far above the minimum wage, which was $1.60. Duties included attendance at the Police

Academy in addition to performing civilian support functions within the department, such as processing criminal history records and parking enforcement.

The cadet program had been a part of the police department for approximately four years before I joined. Its specific intent was to try and boost minority recruitment, particularly blacks, into the ranks of law enforcement. In this regard, the program had been a failure because up to the time of my hiring it had never employed any blacks. It had recruited one Puerto Rican and two Mexicans, but all of the program's other hires had been white.

I still clearly recall my job interview. I sat across the table from the assistant chief of police in charge of personnel (a white man), the captain of the uniformed Patrol Division (a white man), and James Woods, who was the personnel manager for the City of Colorado Springs (a black man and civilian employee).

Mr. Woods took a special interest in me. He had an easygoing personality and was quick with a smile, which belied the fire in him to induce change in a system he knew was inherently biased against and prejudicial toward blacks. He had a passion to "fix" that systemic problem and eagerly pointed out the obstacles that I would be confronting.

"You recognize that there are no blacks in this department. This is lily white. You're going to be up against a lot to make yourself a success. These people don't deal with blacks unless they are arresting them. Would you have any problems interacting in an all-white environment?"

"No. I've been called names before. I can handle it."

"You know Jackie Robinson?" he asked.

"Yes."

"Well the thing about Jackie is that he was successful because he chose not to fight back. He confronted racism with silence. Think you can do that?"

"Yes, I can." I stared Woods straight in the eye when I said this, my chin held high. I knew who I was. I knew my character. I knew what it was like to be called those names, looked at with suspicion, even hate. I'm not the type to keep my mouth shut when someone gets in my face, but I knew I could pick and choose my moments to do battle.

I was asked a series of questions regarding my background growing up in the Mexican border community of El Paso, Texas; in particular, what was it like being a young black man living in a southern state during the height of the civil rights movement of the 1960s. When I was growing up in that time period as a black person, El Paso was a very liberal southern city. We did not experience the volume of rhetoric or violence that was occurring in the Deep South against the civil rights movement. What we had was only what we saw in the evening TV news coverage. In that respect, the civil rights movement for me was not something in my backyard. It was a TV show. My own life was a multicultural mix of Mexicans, blacks, whites. There was a big military presence that was diverse. It was its own little corner of the country, which is not to say it was immune from racial intolerance. I was born in Chicago, and my mother's moving our family to El Paso was the best decision she ever made, as the city was a far cry from the poverty, gangs, and conflict in Chicago's South Side, where I would have come of age if she had not left. My entire life would have been different.

The interview continued, and Woods let the others begin to pepper me with questions. My personal lifestyle was heavily questioned: Was I a womanizer? I was not. Did I like to frequent nightclubs? I wasn't very active in that scene. Was I a heavy drinker? I rarely indulged. Did I use drugs? Only drugs prescribed by a doctor. I had never used any illicit drugs such as marijuana, which for someone my age during that cultural time period was virtually unheard of, and I was vigorously challenged regarding my answer. Had I ever been involved in anything that would bring shame to the department? I had not.

As the interview progressed, the questions got more pointed to include the use of the pejorative "nigger," and as to how I would respond to various scenarios if it were used in reference to me by department personnel or citizens during the discharge of my duties as an officer.

Could I hold my tongue and instinct to lash out at those who crossed the line in this regard? What about my loyalty to the department? Being the sole black, once word got out to the black community that I worked for the department, efforts probably would be made to compromise me by appealing to my sense of "community" with my "black brothers." Could I, the interview panel asked, withstand that pull?

Such questions are racist when viewed in hindsight and in the light of today's laws governing employment interviews. This was 1972, barely three years removed from the time when America's major cities were burning as a result of racially fueled riots over the issue of civil rights and equality for America's black citizens. Though a dying breed, the Black Panther Party, with its racially tinged rhetorical slogans of "Black Power," "Kill Whitey," and "Revolution Has Come, Time to Pick Up the Gun," was still a social force to be reckoned with. For a department that had been "lily white" for much of its history and had not experienced blacks except in an extremely negative context, such questioning from their perspective was deemed to be natural and necessary.

I was asked several times if I could withstand the barrage of scrutiny that would come my way—should I get hired—during the one-year probationary period that would immediately follow, without jeopardizing my job by retaliating against my tormentors.

Again and again they asked in one way or another if I could respond in the same fashion as Jackie Robinson, who did *not* fight back against those who baited him with racial insults and physical assaults during his first year in the big leagues. Could I, they asked, set an example that a black man was just as capable of wearing the uniform of the Colorado Springs Police Department as a white man, and that a man of color deserved to walk among them as an equal?

My answers to their questions were that yes, I could do all that the job asked of me, and would be honored to do it at the same time.

What I didn't tell them was that as a child in the time period when I grew up, the 1960s, we had to literally fight for our self-respect. I was raised by my mother to do just about the opposite of what the CSPD was asking of me. My mother told me that if anyone called me a nigger I had better "knock them in the mouth" and teach them to call us the proper way. As a child I had gotten in three fights with other children who had called me a nigger.

All of those fights resulted in some trouble with school, and I had to speak to my mother about them. She wasn't upset with me, far from it, but she did ask me, "Did you whip their ass?" I always said yes, even though two of those times I was lying to her. I might have been the one who got "whipped," but none of those other kids ever called me a nigger again.

I must have answered their questions to their liking, because I was sworn in as a cadet on November 13, 1972. My first assignment was the far from exciting job of graveyard shift in the Identifications and Records Bureau, filing records and navigating mountains of paperwork. But first I had to receive my uniform.

My cadet uniform consisted of dark brown slacks and a light brown shirt. That was it. A policeman's uniform was dark blue pants and a royal blue shirt. Both shirts had the Colorado Springs logo, and most important, we were required to wear a policeman's cap.

I reported to the lieutenant in charge of equipment and supply requisition, who was responsible for issuing all newly sworn personnel their uniforms and equipment.

At this time, I wore a small Afro hairstyle and the department did not have experience in dealing with anyone wearing an Afro. This lieutenant measured my head size but did not take into account the amount of hair on the top and sides of my head. He deliberately pressed the measuring tape down as deep as he could to my skin, rendering a false hat size, about one and a half sizes too small. When he gave it to me and I tried it on, I told him it was too small and showed it to him on my head. It literally sat on top of my Afro because I could not pull it down over the side of my head. I looked like one of those cartoon monkeys that wears a hat several sizes too small while amusing a crowd, begging for money while the organ grinder plays music.

"You can either wear this cap, or get a haircut," he said to me, then laughed.

I decided to flip his snarky arrogance back at him by taking the hat without any further challenge.

Department policy stated that whenever a person in the uniformed ranks left the building he or she was required to wear his hat. Beginning the very next day, I started leaving the police department to walk the downtown streets in search of a lunchtime eatery. I would put my one-and-a-half-sizes-too-small hat on the top of my Afro-styled head, hold my head up high, and proudly walk down those city streets in my police cadet uniform, looking like a damn clown, acknowledging, with a tip of my cap and a "How d'you do," the funny looks from the people who stared and pointed their fingers at me.

This went on for about a month until one day the chief of police saw me coming back from one of my lunch breaks.

"Why are you wearing your hat like that?" he asked.

"The lieutenant refused to give me one that fit my head and my hairstyle," I said.

The chief ordered me to advise the lieutenant to immediately issue me a hat that fit my head appropriately and that it was a "direct order." I gave the lieutenant that message with a big smile on my face. He was not very happy with it or my obvious enjoyment in delivering it. He asked me the hat size I needed. I told him I didn't know. He angrily went and got a couple of different larger hats, and I finally settled on one that appropriately fit my Afro-styled head. I had beaten him at his own game. Jackie Robinson would have been proud, I think.

There was also another incident that stands out in my mind from my early days as a cadet that's painful to look back on. It occurred during a graveyard shift in the Records Bureau. John, an elderly white I.D. technician, was in a jovial, somewhat frisky mood as we described our ideally attractive favorite female celebrities. He described his fantasy date and I described mine. We went back and forth, with me mentioning a couple of white women who met with his approval. I then mentioned the multitalented, voluptuous, and sultry Lola Falana, then one of the most popular entertainers on the Las Vegas scene. John recognized her name, and the smile that had dominated his face as we bantered back and forth immediately disappeared. His response shocked me because he said he could not relate to my choice in Ms. Falana as "beautiful" because he did not know what constituted beauty in a "colored" woman. After all these many years, I distinctly remember John's next statement to me: "I don't know how *you* people define beauty in a woman." He said this very casually without any intended, overt malice. He stated he had never looked at women of color in terms of physical attractiveness and therefore to describe Lola Falana as "beautiful" was something he could not understand or relate to in any way.

I was dumbfounded to say the least. This nice, elderly man had unknowingly and unintentionally slapped me in the face with his statement. To my nineteen-year-old innocent way of seeing the world, an attractive woman was, well . . . an attractive woman, regardless of skin color. If she had big, seductive eyes, a shapely figure, and a sultry, sensuous demeanor about her—as personified by Ms. Falana—it did not matter if she was black, white, or any other color in the rainbow. My relationship with

John, a man I had looked forward to seeing at work each day, was never the same.

It was during my work in the Records Bureau that I first encountered Arthur, Sgt. Jim, and the other members of the Narcotics Unit. Chuck, the man who would go on to be my double in the Klan investigation, had not yet joined the police department. The narcotics office was located in the basement of the police department, and they would come up to the first-floor office of the Records Bureau requesting criminal histories of suspects they were investigating.

From the start, I was intrigued and fascinated by these unkempt-looking, long-haired "hippies," as they were respectfully called by everyone in the department. I was immediately told to *never* acknowledge their identity in public unless they acknowledged you first, because they could be operating in an undercover capacity and that recognition could jeopardize their investigation and put their lives in danger.

They looked like the bad guys with their long hair, beards, and sloppy street clothes, but they carried guns and enforced the law with the good guys. I wanted to be one of them.

At the bare minimum I was looking at four years before I could hope to entertain the possibility of being considered for a detective position in the Narcotics Unit, and that was only on the chance that there was an opening. And there was one last major obstacle standing in my way: there had never been a black detective in the history of the Colorado Springs Police Department.

After some time the narcotics detectives had gotten accustomed to my presence in the Records Bureau, so I struck up conversations with them—in particular Arthur—about the mechanics of being an undercover cop. I questioned them about every nuance imaginable when they came to my desk for criminal history records requests. I asked about the language of the street, slang terms for drugs, and price ranges in various weight categories. I wanted to know how I should respond in a particular scenario if something out of the ordinary was said. If I heard a drug reference in a movie, I would later question one of them about the factuality of it in practical use. Within a short period of time I had, quite literally, made a pest of myself in their eyes, but in doing so I achieved something much more tangible and important—I had begun to get myself noticed by members of the "good ole boys" network.

It wasn't enough, though, that I had gotten the attention of the Narcotics Unit with my youthful, persistent, and enthusiastic inquiries about their job. The main member of the "good ole boys" whose attention I needed to garner was Arthur, then a sergeant, the head of the Narcotics Unit, and the one whom I saw as my "Moses" with the ticket for me to enter the "promised land."

I peppered the investigating officers in the Narcotics Unit with questions about the day-to-day aspects of the job; Arthur received those too, punctuated with a big exclamatory "Make me a narc!" whenever I saw him in the station.

His response was always the same: he would always smile or emit a hearty laugh, shake his head no, and go on about his business.

Along with pestering the narcs, I quickly fell in love with being a cadet, grunt work and all, and my dreams of being a high school PE teacher were put out of my mind. I loved putting on a uniform each day. I loved the feeling of being a part of a team.

I loved the interaction with the public (although maybe they didn't always love interacting with me as I wrote parking tickets). I even loved filing paperwork and fetching records for the other detectives. It was an environment I had never experienced before in that I was a visible representation of the city, and I had to learn the art of interacting with people from all walks of life. People skills. It's one thing for a teenager to work in a fast-food restaurant, but another to have responsibilities that can affect people's lives. It made me grow up real quick.

When I was working parking enforcement, people would obviously become irate—cuss at me, rail at me, and I had to learn to hold my ground. Actually, if I'm being honest, I probably was more hurt when someone I was writing up a parking citation for would say I wasn't a real cop than I would have been if their anger had turned racial. It was during this time that I came of age. I learned what it takes to be both a cop and a man.

On June 18, 1974, my twenty-first birthday, I was sworn in as a police officer for the City of Colorado Springs, the first black to graduate from the ranks of the Police Cadet program. To say this felt good is an understatement. I had made history in Colorado Springs, and I knew whatever lay ahead was going to be both fulfilling and exciting.

But the ceremony didn't go off without a hitch. I knew early on that I was somewhat of a "rebel" at heart. At my swearing-in ceremony, the other applicant hired, Ralph Sanchez, showed up before the mayor of Colorado Springs wearing a nice suit and tie with a crisp black shirt and spit-shined black shoes. I, on the other hand, wore a nice pair of slacks, sharply pressed (I had been ironing my own clothes—heavily starched—since elementary school), with a dark pullover shirt and a light fall jacket. I didn't like suits and ties, had never liked suits and ties, and had not been told to wear them. The instructions given regarding my appearance for the ceremony were to look "nice," and my appearance, by my standards, was "nice." Besides, in my mind I had passed all of the required tests and was now on the employment rolls of the CSPD. I did not need to impress the mayor of Colorado Springs or anyone else who was going to be present for the ceremony by wearing a suit and tie. Along with the mayor the other attendees consisted of only the three members of the interview panel. My mother was working and could not get the time off to attend.

Ralph's early display of appearance and conformity to the "norm" of CSPD expectations was to set the tone for the career paths he and I were to follow. What started out as a friendship between us because of our mutual endeavors on the road to being police cadets turned sour within a year as he, being six months older, graduated into the ranks of the uniformed Patrol Division sooner and quickly developed an attitude that he was better than I was. He felt he was now my superior and insisted I treat him with deference I was unable to muster. He became a "model patrolman," what we in the department referred to as a "Yes Man" or, in a more crass term, a "Kiss Ass." He was always willing to do the bidding of those in a position to help advance his personal agenda. Ralph always adhered to departmental protocol, never crossing the line or even going near it. To do so in his limited worldview would be to risk upsetting those valuable potential human assets who could push his personal/professional agenda to the next level, so Ralph was not one to push that envelope. It got him nowhere, as he was not liked and was looked down upon by his peers within the department. But within six months of becoming an officer of the CSPD in his suit and tie, Ralph did something truly terrible.

As a patrolman Ralph shot and killed a teenaged boy, a known burglar, in broad daylight. Ralph said the boy was armed and pulled a gun on him while fleeing the scene of one of his burglaries. The problem with Ralph's story was that the individual did not have a weapon on him. It was only through the masterly verbal sleight of hand on the part of the El Paso County district attorney that Ralph survived the shooting investigation through the grand jury. He retained his position as a police officer; however, his credibility among his peers suffered significantly after the incident. He continued his "Yes Man" role in hopes of moving beyond the uniformed ranks but continued to be ignored by those in power.

Although I was a rebel at heart and had a nonconformist personality, I was still savvy enough to know that when conforming to established trends, it was necessary to do certain things that would benefit me personally. In other words I picked my moments to challenge "the system" and figured out how far I could push the envelope. I was never one for the stylized trappings of official police uniform protocol and other such accoutrements.

If I do say so myself, I looked damn good in my uniform; I just didn't like wearing it and didn't want to make a career out of being a patrol officer. Seeing the narcotics officers coming to my office for assistance sowed the seed that grew into my professional aspiration. Becoming an undercover narcotics investigator, someone who looked like the average citizen but who carried a gun and badge and had the authority of the law behind him, became my calling, my professional purpose and direction.

From that moment forward, my every waking moment was dedicated to trying to make that a reality.

Immediately following my swearing-in ceremony and receiving my formal commission, I marched over to Arthur's office and showed him my brand-new city certificate of employment and department identification card signifying my minutes-long status as a full-fledged cop. I then repeated my obnoxious declaration: "Now that I'm legal will you make me a narc?"

He laughed at my audacious persistence and said, "You need to put in at least two years in uniform before consideration. That's just the rules."

Little did I know that my luck would change much more quickly.

For ten months I went about the business of being a patrolman: writing traffic citations, collaring drunks in public, investigating burglaries, robberies, domestic disputes, etc. It wasn't exactly what you'd find on a TV police drama, but for me it was all new and exciting. I still hollered at Arthur each time I saw him with my call "Make me a narc," and one day I got more than a smile and a shake of the head from him.

On that day Arthur asked me, "How'd you like to work an undercover assignment with us, Ron?"

As you can imagine, I didn't hesitate. "Yes!"

"It's Stokely Carmichael. The Black Panther leader is in town giving a speech. We're concerned about the impact he might have. What he might say. We need a black person to go in because our white guys won't fit in very well."

Stokely Carmichael, later known as Kwame Ture, was the

former prime minister of the Black Panther Party and an iconic contemporary member of the civil rights pantheon that included Martin Luther King Jr. and Malcolm X. Carmichael belonged to and later became leader of the SNCC (Student Nonviolent Coordinating Committee), which staged sit-in protests at white-owned businesses that refused service to black citizens in the South. He is the man commonly credited in 1966 with coining the term "Black Power"—the fist-pumping, chest-thumping revolutionary clarion call for black empowerment. The protests associated with the contemporary Black Lives Matter movement are direct descendants of Carmichael's message.

Arthur explained to me that Stokely was contracted to give a speech at a club called Bell's Nightingale. The Nightingale was frequented by blacks, with late-night dancing and live bands. Bell's was in the central part of town—just off of the downtown strip.

We had two black nightclubs in Colorado Springs (Bell's and the Cotton Club), and they were popular in their own right. Duncan's Cotton Club was known as a hangout for pimps and prostitutes—as a police officer we always were told to keep our eye on the Cotton Club, especially on GI payday. Bell's wasn't on the main stretch of downtown but on a side street, so it had less obvious disreputable traffic, you might say.

Although Stokely's speech was open to the public, tickets were set at a reasonable price and were required for admission.

It was presumed that the bulk of Colorado Springs' finest black citizenry, as well as its youthful revolutionaries, would show up in force, hoping to bask in Stokely's feverish antiwhite/problack aura and to taste his past glory, when his words struck fear in the hearts and minds of the highest elements of America's white political power structure.

To the police department, the potential outcome was unpredictable, and so concerned were my superiors that they sought me out after my years of vocally advocating for a chance to be an undercover operative.

Now was my time to prove my professional mettle to them, and it was to be against one of the foremost leaders of the civil rights movement, a man I had watched numerous times as a teenager on the late-night news agitating the system and provocatively confronting the forces I now represented.

The department still had enough respect that Stokely's rhetorical powers of persuasion would be formidable enough that they wanted an "inside" observer to his performance and the audience response to his message. They were concerned that his message would resonate to such a degree that it might rekindle the emotional fervor of the local black masses and possibly lead to a violent response. Although it was never spoken, I knew Arthur and the department brass were worried Stokely would ignite another city—our city—on fire, much like the 1967 riots. My assignment was to monitor his speech, gauge audience reaction, and report on possible response procedures the department should take steps to enact to prevent any trouble.

On the night of the speech, I reported to the basement office of the Narcotics Unit dressed in casual clothes suitable for an evening of "nightclubbing." I wore a leisure suit with bell-bottoms. I had to have a blazer on to conceal my gun. Flared, open collar—very *Saturday Night Fever.*

While I was being taped up with a wireless body transmitter so my surveillance backup officers could listen in on my end of the conversation, I was bombarded by various members of the

unit with what-if scenarios, which was my crash course in undercover work.

What if the suspect offers you some cocaine to snort, how
do/should/would you respond?

Answer: Do not take. Say you're not in the mood right now,
but thanks. Be cool, but ask around who's selling. If we can make
a drug bust later, all the better.

What if you're asked to smoke a joint, how do/should/would
you respond?

Answer: Same as your response to cocaine.

What if someone pulls a gun on you, how do/should/would
you respond?

Answer: This one is a bit more complicated. The main thing
if someone draws a gun on you, which has happened to me on
a few occasions, is to always remember you are wired for
sound. Officers are listening to you and you're not alone.
Start communicating to the officers. Say to your assailant if you
can, "Oh, that's an interesting gun you got pointed at my chest.
What kind of gun is that? A blue steel Magnum with six bullets
in it?" That way you've described to your listening officers that
a gun is involved in the situation, it's being pointed in your direction, and trouble has arrived.

Only as a last resort should you take matters into your own
hands. Stay calm, there is backup on the way.

Other officers were schooling me on the various prices for
different quantities of drugs and giving me a crash course in the
underground language of the drug scene. It was obvious the
narcs were anxious about an inexperienced brother officer going
into an unknown environment.

Arthur, meanwhile, was counting one hundred dollars of

official city funds and recording the serial numbers in anticipation of a drug transaction possibly taking place, which might result in an arrest. After going through this ritual, I was given a receipt to sign, transferring the money into my official custody and making me responsible for its expenditure and/or return.

I was experiencing a massive case of sensory overload, which, for me, was very exhilarating. I was a virtual human sponge, soaking up every bit of information that my mind, young both in age and police experience, could absorb, while trying to retain as much as possible, though not necessarily succeeding.

My final marching orders were to concentrate on Stokely Carmichael and his speech, with emphasis on the audience response to his message. I was told if the opportunity presented itself I was to feel free to make a drug purchase, as long as I was able to somehow identify the seller. As a new cop accustomed to strict rules of conduct governing all manner of behavior, I asked what was to me arguably the most important question of all: Could I order an alcoholic drink while in the bar?

Everyone laughed at the naive innocence of my question—one I later learned was common to newly assigned members of the Narcotics Unit—but Arthur eased my concern by telling me one mixed drink or beer was acceptable, as long as it was in keeping with the need of the investigation. I should always be aware that what I did and said would be used in court, and any consumption of a substance thoroughly looked into during a trial.

I was given an unmarked car, with a portable radio, and made my way to Bell's Nightingale. In the early evening hours, there was already an overflow of parked cars. Clearly Stokely's much anticipated talk was going to be a local success. After paying my three-dollar entry fee for the program, "Stokely Carmichael Speaks," I made my way through the crowd. I started to get the standard "stomach butterflies" knowing that I was operating in an undercover capacity, not to mention I had already recognized several people whom I had, over the course of my young career, cited for various traffic offenses. I also recognized several of our local "ghetto celebrities," pimps, their prostitutes, and drug dealers. A couple of the younger, more "thuggish" elements were also within eyesight. I felt like Daniel entering the lion's den, food waiting to be recognized and consumed.

All of the people gathered for Carmichael's speech had an inherent dislike for the police, and it was only exacerbated when a black officer was concerned. To them I was *not* a "black" man, but rather a police officer who happened to be black. In their eyes I was a "traitor" to the cause for which a black revolutionary brother like Stokely had dedicated his life and was here to speak about. Where black brothers like Stokely were intent on bringing down the white man—a "devil" in their eyes—and his racist-centered society and dominant government structure, brothers like me were caught in a netherworld common to black officers, a "phantom-like" void in which we were too black for the white community we served as well as some of our fellow officers, and too "blue," for the color of the uniform we wore, for our fellow "soul brothers" steeped in the cause of civil rights/ social revolution beneficial for the black community. But a good many of our fellow citizens of color did not tend to view black officers through the jaded lens of suspicion or consider us lost sheep who had strayed from the herd. Rather they saw they shared with black police officers the commonality of a shared life experience built on a background of biased degradation based on skin pigmentation and other social factors.

But to black revolutionaries like Stokely, because I and others like me had chosen to wear a badge, gun, and blue uniform representative of the forces of an "oppressive" (their point of view) government and enforce what they perceived to be naturally unjust laws specifically designed to work against those victimized by that oppression, we had become modern-day "house slaves"—house niggers, each of us a black Judas who had chosen to collaborate with the governmental "massa" (master) and enforce the "white man's justice." We had become slaves to the "system," the white man's "boy," as I was called on many occasions during my career by my self-proclaimed black "brothers."

Now, I was proud of being both black and a cop. I was proud of my blackness without being angry. I was in awe of Stokely because he was a figure of the civil rights movement. People like him (MLK, Malcolm X, Rosa Parks, Recy Taylor, John Lewis, and so forth) made life better for people like me. But now here I was being thrust into this unique situation, and I had no qualms because I could differentiate being a cop who was black and a black man in white America.

The club was peppered with a smattering of whites, those "wannabe" blacks known as "wiggers"—"white niggers"—by today's hip-hop community.

I happened to find a table near the back of the bar with a lone occupant, a fairly attractive German lady. With her permission, I took a seat with my back to the wall, a common strategic move by undercover operatives—and police in general—having a view of the entire location in case an altercation erupted. From this position, I also took note of the closest exit in case I had to make a hasty escape.

She welcomed my company and eagerly struck up a conversation in heavily German-accented English. Her conversation was flirtatious in nature and put me in a slightly awkward position because I had just started to date the woman who, five years later, would become my wife. Although we were not yet in any committed relationship, I knew in my heart—though I hadn't told her yet—I wanted to pursue the relationship as far as it and she would allow. In spite of this, the "dog" in me—all men have a little "dog" in them where women are concerned, especially if they are as I was, a fraction over twenty-one years of age, single, with no personal obligations of any kind—was somewhat flattered by the German woman's interest in me. I, however, was far too disciplined and dedicated to my goal to allow her flirtatious interest in a possible amorous adventure to derail my purpose. That was a line I had no intention of crossing.

I ordered a rum and Coke, my first alcoholic drink while on duty, and graciously refilled what she was drinking. I redirected her conversational interest in me to the topic of drugs. She offered to "score" (buy or introduce me to someone with drugs for sale) some marijuana or cocaine for us to enjoy, but before I could delve deeper into this prospect, Stokely Carmichael was introduced to a rousing standing ovation complete with the symbolic raised, closed fist of the Black Power segment of the civil rights movement and shouts of "Right on, brother" and "Black Power." The crowd was fully in the moment with him.

I, however, while clapping, was busy laughing at my female companion joining in with the crowd in her thick German accent yelling "Black Power" with a raised white fist.

Stokely's talk was typical of the many he had given over the years. It was laced with references to his philosophical beliefs in Pan-Africanism, an ideological movement that encouraged worldwide economic, social, and political solidarity among people of the African diaspora. It was—is—a belief based on a shared historical legacy united by a common enemy: the white race. Coupled with his belief in a Marxist revolutionary overthrow of the American political system, Stokely's message was of great interest to the black masses and concern to my superiors.

Stokely was dynamic, mesmerizing. The alternating effect of his pitch and tone could raise the audience into a fevered frenzy or bring them down, as if they were listening to a soothing Sunday morning sermon. He was like a master puppeteer, pulling the strings on our emotions and leading us down a path that we probably never knew we wanted to tread.

I found myself—several times—caught up in the rapture of his reasoning against the very governmental institution I represented and the white people I generally looked on with fondness and good intentions. When these occasions occurred and I found myself enthusiastically clapping and yelling "Right on, brother," I had to quickly remind myself that we were in adversarial roles and sincerely hope and pray that I was a good enough undercover actor that my surveillance officers listening to the wireless body transmitter would not be able to detect in my voice the tone of agreement with and acceptance of his logic.

Stokely, with the audience, me included, in the palm of his rhetorical hand, blasted the white man and the white race by stating that throughout their history they had understood only one thing exceptionally well—the power that comes from the barrel of a gun. He then called for the black masses in America to arm themselves to prepare for the "BIG" revolution that was soon to come. This one statement received, perhaps, the greatest applause response from the crowd and the loudest verbal affirmation in the form of "Right on, brother" and "Black Power."

At the end of his nearly forty-five-minute presentation, Stokely was given a standing ovation and further shouts of black affirmation from the crowd. His Bell's Nightingale hosts then formed a receiving line for him to meet and greet his many admirers and those who simply wanted to touch a living, breathing piece of contemporary black history. I stood in the line and slowly made my way toward him. When I finally got within reach, I was struck by the regal grandeur of his physical being.

Up close, Stokely stood approximately six foot four with flawless cocoa-colored skin. As I shook his hand he gave me one of his warm, infectious smiles with the whitest, most flawless teeth I had ever seen. I thought to myself, *This is a pretty good-looking man.*

As we shook hands, I asked him if he truly believed an armed conflict between the black and white races was inevitable. He squeezed my hand tighter and pulled my face closer to his, eyes quickly darted around the room as he whispered, "Brother, arm yourself and get ready because the revolution is coming and we're gonna have to kill whitey. Trust me, it is coming."

He then pulled back and thanked me for coming to hear him speak. He wished me well, as I did him, and my first undercover assignment and brush with history came to an end.

I left the nightclub and headed back to the station with my

team. We debriefed, and I told them what took place inside. They had been listening, so they knew what Stokely had said, but I talked about the atmosphere. How it was just electric, exciting, but not angry despite the content of the speech. He was not inciting immediate violence. I filed the necessary reports and went home that night feeling exhilarated.

At that moment my professional life could not have been better. I had worked my way up to become a uniformed patrolman on a special assignment with the narcotics unit. In three months' time I would officially become an undercover narcotics detective, the first black in the history of the Colorado Springs Police Department and, as I later learned, the youngest— by about a month.

So I began my undercover career investigating the Black Panthers, but now it was time to go after the other side of the coin. The Klan had called, after all.

3

I'M THE VOICE, YOU'RE THE FACE

There are certain truths about undercover work that must be acknowledged. First, I broke the most basic rule of all and that was going into a case without a plan of operation. Second, I used my real name instead of my undercover identity—a cardinal sin. Third, having used my real name, I gave the undercover address and phone number without anticipating the possibility that anything would come of the effort.

When this investigation began I had been a police officer for four years, three of which had been spent working undercover narcotics and vice. I was well versed in the basics of how to conduct such investigations; however, in this particular instance I was much too lackadaisical in my initial approach when looking into this matter, and my lapsed judgment allowed me to make a critical error. Fortunately, the people I was dealing with were not, to use an old adage, "the brightest bulbs in the socket," and my mistakes did not jeopardize the outcome of the investigation. If anything, my failings at the onset, unknown to me, were the seeds of its success.

After getting off the phone with Ken, I immediately contacted my sergeant, Ken Trapp. I told Trapp I wanted to use Chuck, in undercover narcotics, to assist me. Ken was on board, and so I contacted Arthur, who had been promoted to lieutenant in the period between Stokely and the Klan investigation, and requested Chuck's use for an undercover assignment on November 9. I gave him the details and what I hoped to accomplish with an investigation.

This was to be an intelligence investigation whose purpose would be to learn as much about the growing threat of the Klan in Colorado Springs, and Colorado in general, and to prevent any acts of terror that might result. Anytime during the course of the investigation we could have brought it to an end by arresting several Klansmen for misdemeanor offenses; however, this was not my objective. Had these individuals strayed into the realm of felony offenses we most definitely would have taken them down and brought an end to the investigation. Until that bridge was crossed, I was determined to follow the intelligence trail as far as it would take me and learn as much as possible about the Colorado Springs chapter of the Ku Klux Klan. Now Arthur was a narcotics investigator, and his investigations were intended to result in arrests and gathering evidence for trial. Gathering intelligence was something he did not understand or want to do.

He refused my request.

"Not only do I not have the manpower for this, but the second this Ken hears one of our white officers speaking to him, he'll know he's been speaking to a black man on the phone."

"What does a black man talk like?" I asked.

"Well, you know . . ." Arthur trailed off.

"No, I don't know. Explain it to me."

I was met with dead silence. I had heard this from a few other officers I worked with too. They were blinded by mental prejudices and stereotypes about speech patterns of black Americans of African descent. They treated me like in that scene in *Airplane!* when June Cleaver stands up and speaks jive, which was what many of them meant by the phrase "talk like a black man." Another colleague told me when I asked that same question, "You know, shucking and jiving and saying 'fuck you' and 'motherfucker' all the time." I immediately burst into laughter at the incongruity of his statement as to its meaning and how that meaning concerned me in the context of the potential success of this investigation.

Arthur and others in the department who had shared these thoughts were essentially saying I would not be able to successfully communicate with these Klansmen over the phone. Being a black man, I would ultimately "shuck and jive" during my conversation, thereby giving away that I was in fact a "black" man; I would, in essence, somehow give in to the urge to say "fuck" and "motherfucker," and any Klansman I might be speaking with would immediately know he was talking to a "black" man.

Just ridiculous, and in its own way, hilarious at the same time in its absurdity.

His second reason for refusing my request was that this whole idea of the Ku Klux Klan being in Colorado Springs was not to be taken seriously and he would not allow the identification of one of his undercover investigators to be irresponsibly compromised over such foolishness. To him, the ad was a prank at best, and Ken just an angry man no one should worry about.

With the lieutenant's rejection, I again consulted with Sergeant Trapp, and I made the decision to go over Arthur's head directly to the chief of police to secure the resources I would need to follow up on the proposed meeting with the local Klan organizer. Sergeant Trapp supported me fully. In terms of my career, this decision was not what one would call a wise one. In regard to the acrimonious relationship I had with Lieutenant Arthur, this major step up the chain of command—bypassing a captain and assistant chief of detectives—was sure to fan the flames of that animosity.

The animosity between Arthur and me had developed when I worked for him in narcotics about one year earlier. He was a mentor to me prior to this. Essentially there was a decision that had to be made on a narcotics case and we all took a vote on proposals presented by Arthur and the sheriff's supervisor. I voted in favor of the sheriff's position, much to Arthur's chagrin and anger. He felt that as a CSPD officer I should have sided with him and the city sergeant in the dispute. He did not like the fact that I had expressed my independent mind on an issue against him. From that point forward in our professional relationship, nothing was ever the same between us.

I had only one week to put events in motion for the meeting with the local Klan organizer and quite frankly did not have time to worry about inflaming existing bitter feelings or about department-rank protocol and the damage resulting from banged-up egos. My bottom line was that the lieutenant had issues with me and he would continue to have issues with me, regardless of whether I did this or not. In other words, I had nothing to lose.

Another aspect to the fuel I was about to add to this personal fire between us concerned the lieutenant's attitude toward our chief of police. He intensely resented the chief, having no respect for him whatsoever because of the politics of his ascension to that rank.

The chief had been promoted only a short time ago and, up to this point, had previously held the permanent civil-service rank of lieutenant, though he was junior in seniority to Arthur, his narcotics counterpart. As a lieutenant, the chief had been in charge of the department's Community Relations Division, considered a nondescript job within the police hierarchy, and had been quite good at it. Because he had not served in a "front-line" capacity in the same vein as one of his "peers" in the detective or uniformed patrol division, the chief was vilified for having leapfrogged them in the selection process. In their eyes he was deemed unqualified to be chief of police of the Colorado Springs Police Department.

Arthur, the narcotics lieutenant, failed to come to grips with the reality that time had passed him by. During that period the CSPD, like many police departments in the country, began requiring a more educated status for advancement within its rank structure. Traditional issues, such as being more deserving (am I better qualified based on case productivity and seniority) were no longer the paradigm on which a promotional consideration was based. They were being relegated to a secondary status in favor of personal achievement in higher education. One of the specific requisites the promotional board sought when searching for a new police chief was that candidate from within the current rank structure possess at least a bachelor's degree. The narcotics lieutenant held an associate's degree compared to the Community Relations lieutenant, who possessed a master's degree, the only ranking officer in the CSPD with a postgraduate degree at the time.

Sergeant Trapp and I briefed the chief on the action I had taken thus far: the mailed response to the newspaper ad, the telephone conversation with the local Klan organizer, and his stated plans to burn crosses to announce their presence to city residents. The Klan desired to perpetrate a historical act of domestic terrorism, thus increasing white pride and consequentially boosting enrollment numbers.

He expressed great interest in our briefing and after a few questions asked if I needed any additional manpower. I requested the use of two surveillance detectives to accompany me on November 9. He then phoned the lieutenant and directed him to give me all the necessary manpower assistance I needed to move this investigation forward.

As expected, Arthur was not pleased by my actions. I, as expected, did not care whether his feelings and ego were upset. In my mind this meeting was a unique opportunity to create an opening into a group with a long history of domestic terrorism that was now in the process of establishing itself in my city.

I held my first meeting with Chuck and briefed him on everything involving the investigation.

I told him what I had done. The nature of the phone call, and what Ken and I had discussed.

"They are planning burnings, white-only charity drives, recruitment efforts, and we need to know what else."

He started laughing. "A black cop infiltrating the Klan? This is nuts. Won't they know that you're black?"

"That's why we're going to be on the exact same page. I'll be listening to everything you and he say through the mic. And you'll be aware of everything I say to him on the phone. I'm the voice, you're the face."

"This is just about the craziest thing I've heard. I'm in," said Chuck through his wide smile.

Unfortunately, Chuck's availability was very limited, because of both his narcotic workload and department politics, and he could be used only as a last resort, so I would need to continue the bulk of the deception via the telephone; thus, we needed to stay in sync in terms of any conversation between us individually and any member of The Organization.

The November 9 meeting was pivotal because Ken had already formed a tentative positive image of "Ron Stallworth" based on the initial phone conversation. I informed Chuck that he had one immediate challenge: take that positive image I had planted in Ken's mind through the telephone interaction and reinforce it during the face-to-face meeting.

As I explained to Chuck, Ken always had to maintain the belief that he was dealing with one person, whether when talking to me on the phone or to him (Chuck) in person; we needed to coordinate our conversations so we could pick up from one encounter to the next without any breaks in conversational flow.

If I had a telephone conversation that led to a face-to-face meeting, which Chuck attended pretending to be me, he had to know every aspect of that conversation so he could be prepared to discuss any issues associated with it should they arise. By the same token, every face-to-face conversation he had with the Klansmen, I had to know every detail. In other words, the conversations Chuck and I had with these individuals had to match in order to fool them.

On November 7, two days before our scheduled meeting, I phoned Ken to confirm our meeting in two days in Security. We agreed that the hippie-looking white guy and I would meet at 7:00 P.M. in the parking lot of the Kwik Inn diner.

Ken was relaxed enough to reveal that because of the publicity regarding the newspaper recruitment ad, the Army had placed him on leave until his military tour of duty ended in thirty-seven days. I noted that the Army's recognizing Ken from a classified ad with no name or identifying information attached wouldn't be possible. If he was actually on probation for his involvement with the Klan, the Army must have found out about something else.

But the Klan was on a publicity blitz, it seemed. The *Gazette Telegraph,* one of two main Colorado Springs papers, had an article announcing David Duke, Grand Wizard of the KKK, would be coming to our town for an appearance—just a little item in the paper.

"There was also an article this week about David Duke coming to Colorado Springs soon. This true?" I asked Ken.

"Yes, Duke personally telephoned the newspaper and told them he would be in the city in January," Ken said. "We're going to hold a big rally. We have six robed members right now, and are looking to add more. A real announcement. We're still confirming the schedule with David, but you'll be the first to know, Ron."

We chatted some more, mostly pleasantries and small talk, and then Ken said, "Well, I gotta go. But see you in two days."

On the night of the ninth, I met with Chuck and another narcotics investigator, Jimmy, to get ready. We went over the course of action, with Chuck driving up to the Kwik Inn, and Jimmy and I in a van just across the street in range.

Chuck had been fitted with a wireless body transmitter that allowed me to listen to and record his conversation. In addition, I gave Chuck personal items of identification—just in case they were asked for—to confirm his identity as "Ron Stallworth."

Those items included a library card, credit cards, Social Security card—anything bearing my name that did not have my picture or otherwise identify me as a black man.

Chuck brought a gun, concealed, which is standard in undercover work. Even if he was going to get patted down by Ken and his associates, he could say he always carried a weapon.

We drove over to the diner, with Chuck pulling in under the bright fluorescent lights, Jimmy and I across the street, and then we did what all investigators do at the beginning of a sting. We waited.

4

MY NEW FRIEND DAVID

Our wait wasn't long. Ten minutes after our arriving at the Kwik Inn a truck pulled up and the weird-looking hippie with a Fu Manchu mustache we'd been waiting for got out. He walked over to Chuck's car, and tapped on the window.

"You Ron?" he asked.

"Yes," said Chuck.

"I'm Butch. I'm here to take you to Ken, who's at another location. Come on, get in my car and I'll take you to him."

As with any undercover meeting, it is imperative that the "UC" (undercover operative) do everything he can to maintain control of events to the best of his ability. This is essential not only for his own personal safety and the overall success of the operation but also for the benefit of the surveillance officers, whose primary responsibility is to provide backup for him in the event the situation breaks down and threatens his personal well-being. With this in mind, recognizing that he was "wired for sound" and also had a handheld police radio in his unmarked undercover car, Chuck put up the best fight he could.

"How about I follow you in my car?" Chuck asked.

"No. That's not how this is going to work. You're going to leave your car here, and I'll take you to Ken."

"Well, where are you taking me?"

"You'll see."

Chuck finally relented and got into Butch's truck.

As he entered, Chuck glanced in the direction where Jimmy and I were parked. Because the wireless body transmitter is a one-way device (transmit not receive), we could hear Chuck but could not transmit messages to him. He did not even know if the transmitter was working, though we had tested it after affixing it to his body prior to leaving the office for this meeting. It wasn't uncommon for these devices to have unexpected breakdowns, sometimes in the middle of an undercover operation. As with any such operation, the UC often functioned in a sort of eerie darkness, devoid of knowledge as to whether the transmitter was operating properly and his surveillance was able to clearly hear his conversation, or whether they had any knowledge as to his whereabouts when, as in this instance, he was moving from one location to another without any foreknowledge.

As it turned out, our concerns were unwarranted as Butch drove about a mile and a half to a popular hangout for the local adult crowd, especially the area's military personnel, the Corner Pocket Lounge. A real dive bar with a neon sign, frayed pool tables, and cheap beer. I later learned that the lounge was the "unofficial" recruitment point for Ken and his Ku Klux Klan cohorts. Jimmy and I parked just outside the bar and radioed to surrounding officers our location. Fortunately, on this occasion, the body transmitter was working flawlessly.

Chuck was greeted by Ken—a short (about five foot nine),

stocky (approximately 220 pounds) man about twenty-eight years of age with brown hair cut military length, and a slight mustache. With him was a younger man (approximately twenty) who Butch introduced as his younger brother, Baron. Believing he was talking to me, Ken told Chuck, "I've been impressed talking to you over the telephone. I feel you have some fine ideas that could possibly help The Cause." He then showed Chuck a packet of papers, which he said had all of the necessary information Chuck would need if he decided to join The Cause. He proceeded into an explanation as to his motivation for joining the Ku Klux Klan.

The Klan, according to Ken, became his "salvation" after he had once been shot by some "niggers," and his wife had been raped by several of them. His prejudices toward "niggers," he said, had really begun after he joined the U.S. Army. "Have you been reading the publicity the Klan has been receiving in all the papers?" Ken asked Chuck. Chuck replied yes, though he admitted he probably had missed some of the articles on occasion. Ken went on to explain that he and other Klansmen had been placing these articles, calling journalists. The Klan was making its presence known. It was amateurish, desperate even, but they did get some modest coverage. By being in the press they were hoping to gain sympathy in the public's eye, attract new members, gain attention, and legitimize their Cause. Even though Ken's Klan here was small, it was sensational. The press would cover them no matter what.

Ken explained that the media, in his opinion, had made The Cause look bad and in the process him as well, but he wouldn't elaborate on exactly how the media made him look bad. He'd been having trouble with his military command ever since, and his effort to reenlist was in jeopardy as a result. It was clear from my phone conversations with Ken that he was angry, but now listening to him with Chuck this anger was all the more prominent. There was a distinct rage deep in his voice, at once spiteful and sad, that fueled him.

"What these niggers do needs to be known. Take what happened to Butch's wife," said Ken. Ken stated that Butch's wife had recently been stabbed by "niggers" and the woman who lived on his street was a suspect in the stabbing. He said "someone" had burned a cross on this woman's lawn to send her a message but had done a poor job of it. Later, I checked all police and sheriff's department report databases on this alleged incident and could find no indication that it, in fact, had occurred. If it had, then the victim did not report it to the police . . . a highly unlikely prospect.

Ken's voice changed, as if expressing some pleasant daydream, saying, "I'd like to meet whoever was responsible for the burning so I could show him the correct way to burn a cross and also congratulate him."

Ken went on to explain that Butch was his bodyguard but that the Klan—collectively—was a nonviolent group. He emphasized this point stating, "No form of violence is to be performed unless it is first brought on a member of the group."

Butch, for the first time since arriving at the Corner Pocket Lounge, spoke to Chuck, saying, "In public the Klan is to be referred to as The Organization or The Cause." He explained his personal anguish at wanting to express himself violently in his relationship with "niggers," yet denying himself that opportunity and satisfaction because he always remembered the nonviolent policies of The Organization. "It's hard to hold back sometimes, you know? But The Cause is more important. The plans we have will really change the world."

"Well, I'm certainly interested in joining The Organization," said Chuck.

Ken told him to open the packet of papers and take out the membership application. He explained step-by-step how to fill out the application, including the costs. The fee for the remaining year's dues would be ten dollars, with a full year being thirty dollars. There would also be a fifteen-dollar local chapter fee. Ken identified the bank in which the Klan held an account and told Chuck it would be necessary to attach a picture with the application.

"Butch and I are anxious for you to join The Organization as soon as possible. If you do, in all likelihood you and Baron would be going to Denver soon to become sworn members of the group at the same time." He explained that once the application process was completed it generally took ten days to two weeks to get the membership card returned from the national office in Louisiana.

"So what exactly are the Klan's plans in Colorado Springs?" asked Chuck.

"Cross burnings. Four of them."

"Where?" asked Chuck.

"We're still planning exactly where, but up on the hills around town. Make a real presence."

Butch explained that each cross would be seventeen feet high by eight feet wide and assembled days in advance prior to the burning. Several days before the burning, the members would go to the predetermined locations and dig the holes for the placement of the crosses and then cover them up with rocks until ready for use.

On the night of the burning the members would go to each selected area, remove the rocks, and place the crosses in their respective holes. After dousing the crosses with a flammable solution, a fuse consisting of a lit cigarette placed on a pack of matches was timed to ignite within three minutes, allowing for their getaway.

"I saw that cigarette fuse in a James Bond movie," Ken said proudly.

"Smart," said Chuck. I smiled at Jimmy when I heard this. Couple of 007s we had on our hands.

"If you get your membership approved in enough time you can join us," said Butch.

Ken then continued the narrative regarding the planned activities by telling Chuck they were going to put together a "Poor White Folks Christmas" next month. The members were going to put gift bags of food and other items together for poor white people.

"Niggers," said Ken, "look at Christmas as a time to rip off white people, and the Jews look at it as a time to make money off the white population. No one ever looks out for the welfare of white people, so the members are going to do something for poor white people at Christmas."

Ken warned Chuck to never admit having participated in any cross burnings and never admit to having participated in any acts of violence. This, he explained, was a policy of The Organization.

When asked what the procedure was for introducing another prospective member into The Organization, Ken replied, "The first thing to consider was if there was any Jew" in the prospective member's background. If not then a personal interview—much like this—would be arranged.

I smiled at Jimmy next to me in the surveillance car as we listened. Chuck was thinking two steps ahead, already wondering how we could get another man in there with him.

"As you know, in January David Duke is coming for a rally," said Ken.

In honor of his visit, the Colorado Springs chapter of The Organization was planning a membership march along one of the main downtown streets. The march would be coordinated by the state leader (a Lakewood, Colorado, firefighter), Fred Wilkens. The Organization's objective for Duke's visit was to have a hundred "robed" members, Klansmen in white hooded robes ready to participate in the march in a show of support, in honor of and respect for the Grand Wizard, and to demonstrate that the the Klan was a viable presence in Colorado.

Ken indicated that if they were able to gather the hundred robed members from the Colorado Springs chapter by Christmas, they would possibly be joined by fellow members from Louisiana, Kentucky, the metropolitan Denver area, and several southern Colorado cities, including Pueblo and Canon City, which is home to the state maximum security prison.

"It'll really be something," said Ken.

After a few more minutes of small talk, Chuck took the packet of papers from Ken with the promise to complete the application process and get it in the mail in the next few days. He and Ken agreed to talk further on the subject, and walked to Butch's car in the lot, where they shook hands and parted ways. As they rode back Chuck asked Butch about the number of Klan members in Colorado Springs.

Butch replied that he did not know and he believed only the state organizer, Fred Wilkens, knew how many were in the

Colorado Springs area. He did say that when Chuck got his membership card it would have on it two letters—*CO*—which stood for Colorado, followed by a series of numbers. The first two numbers would be the year and the remaining numbers represented the state membership.

Butch further explained that the Colorado Springs Klan chapter, as in other cities, was divided into "dens" consisting of approximately five members. These were people who, according to Butch, "really trusted each other and socialized together after meetings." He expressed his hope that Chuck, once accepted as a member, could belong to their den.

Chuck was returned to his car at the Kwik Inn parking lot and Butch promised to telephone him in a few days to make sure he had followed up with the membership application. We had two surveillance cars follow Butch back to the Corner Pocket Lounge, where he picked up Baron and Ken. They followed Butch's truck to a nearby house, the occupants of which were later determined to be a Fort Carson Army couple from Watsonville, California. Chuck, Jimmy, and I returned to the station, where we debriefed.

This was solely my investigation; I did not report to Arthur, who was the lieutenant in charge of the Narcotics Unit. To Arthur's credit, I did not feel his animosity toward me had anything to do with my race, but instead had everything to do with my boldness. He had, after all, given me my start working undercover, but a year earlier, we were working a case that involved the sheriff's department. The sheriff's department presented one plan of action for the case, and Arthur presented his own. I sided with the sheriff's department, because I believed it was a better plan. To Arthur this was a betrayal, and our relationship had soured since then. The conflict arose because Arthur demanded loyalty at all costs and I had expressed my independent mind.

Inside the packet of materials Ken had given Chuck were a couple copies of the Klan newspaper, *The Crusader,* and a membership application.

I completed all of the necessary information on the membership application—including filling in my personal data. I also took a photo of Chuck—as required—seated in the office, for submission with the application. We cracked a few jokes about saying cheese for the Klan.

The next day, I obtained ten dollars of department funds from Sergeant Trapp to apply toward the membership fee and mailed the application to Metairie, Louisiana, national headquarters of David Duke's Knights of the Ku Klux Klan.

It's important for me to explain just who David Duke was and is, a man whose name to this day is synonymous with hate and a lightning rod in the current political and media landscape. A man who would soon consider me a "friend."

Though he held the title of Grand Wizard, David Duke could equally lay claim to being called a public relations wizard. He sold his "product" of a "new" Klan during appearances on the early morning and late night talk shows, in *Time* and *Newsweek* magazine articles regarding the transformation of the Klan, and in a host of other media publications, including soft porn magazines such as *Playboy* and *Oui.*

His appearance was that of an all-American boy every mother would want as a prom date for her daughter. He was always well groomed, well mannered (at least in public), articulate, and highly educated, with a master's degree. His Dr. Jekyll appearance belied a Mr. Hyde personality and perspective on racial matters common to the core of America's social and political climate. Publicly he would not talk about hate but about heritage and history. He spawned a new racism for the right-wing masses, one that melded the antipathy to blacks and other minorities to general dissatisfaction with government and fear of an ever-changing complex world.

As he stated in a *Oui* magazine article circa 1979, "I'm not preaching white supremacy," though he has said he firmly believes whites to be superior to blacks and other minorities. "I'm preaching white separatism. I'd like to see all the blacks go back to Africa where they belong, but I'd even be willing to give them part of this country—a couple of states, maybe—as long as they have a separate society."

Duke upgraded his approach to propaganda by "professional-izing" it. He avoided wearing his Klan robe in public media appearances, preferring a suit and tie instead. He personally avoided using derogatory epithets to refer to blacks in public, in particular the word "nigger," and encouraged his followers to do the same when representing the Klan and presenting their case to an audience. In essence, he mainstreamed the Klan, making it seem an acceptable and viable alternative for those looking for a means to express their displeasure with the status quo of their lives and government representatives.

In 1979 Duke, who while in college at Louisiana State University was known to be involved in the neo-Nazi movement parading around campus wearing Nazi-like uniforms, ran for a

Louisiana State Senate seat as a conservative Democrat and won 26 percent of the vote. In 1988 he did, in fact, run in the Democratic primaries for president but failed to get on the ticket. He then sought to gain the nomination from the Populist Party and was successful. Accordingly, he appeared on the ballot for president in eleven states and was a write-in candidate in a few others. Shortly thereafter he changed his political party affiliation from Democratic to Republican. In 1989, he ran for and won a seat as Louisiana state representative in District 89. The following year he ran unsuccessfully for the Republican nomination for U.S. senator from Louisiana. In 1991, Duke ran unsuccessfully for governor of Louisiana. In 1992, he made another unsuccessful presidential primary run, this time as a Republican. In 1996, he made another unsuccessful attempt at a U.S. Senate seat. Finally, in a 1999 special election to replace U.S. Representative Bob Livingston, Duke ran unsuccessfully as a Republican against David Vitter.

It can be argued that all of Duke's campaigns were successful in the sense that they gave him a vast public platform from which to spout his philosophy and racist ideological agenda. This, in turn, forced his campaign opponents to respond, thus making for an often chaotic outpouring of Populist rants in support of Duke and liberal responses against what they perceived to be a neo-Nazi version of Adolf Hitler in a white robe. It made for a lively discussion. Had Duke not been on the ticket in these races much, if not all, of his topical agenda would probably never have been an issue for debate. The fact that he won an election as a Republican after failing twice as a Democratic candidate says a lot about the mind-set of the electorate. The conservative right-wing Republican political agenda was then and still is much more in sync with white, hate-fueled racist extremist groups like the Ku Klux Klan.

The day after the Corner Pocket Lounge meeting I had my first telephone conversation with the Grand Wizard himself.

While reading one of the Klan pamphlets Chuck was given I noticed an advertisement for "The Voice of the Klan" to be reached by calling a Palm Harbor, Florida, phone number. When I phoned, I quickly learned that the "Voice of the Klan" was, in fact, several prerecorded messages from various sections of the country expressing KKK propaganda. The messages were typical of white supremacist rhetoric:

"Wake up, white man! The black man wants your woman and job. The Jew wants your money. The Zionist Occupied Government [ZOG] wants to take away your citizenship rights guaranteed under the U.S. Constitution and make you slaves to all mud people and their Jewish masters. Your only means of salvation is to join the Knights of the Ku Klux Klan, the only group of patriots dedicated to preserving your heritage and rightful place in a white American society."

ZOG was the typical white supremacist reference to the United States and their belief that it was dominated by and under the control of Jews influenced by the policies of Israel. "Mud people" was their reference to any dark-skinned, nonwhite person they considered under the dominion of Jews.

As the expected recorded voice droned on, preaching hate, a voice broke in and said, "Hello."

"Hello?" I asked. "Who is this?"

"This is David Duke, the actual voice of the Klan." He chuckled at this.

I have to say, I was quite surprised.

"I'm Ron Stallworth. I'm one of the new chapter members in Colorado Springs."

"Pleased to meet you."

We exchanged pleasantries, and I let him know how much I admired his leadership and fearlessness. He responded well to being sucked up to.

"Mr. Duke, is it true you're planning a trip in January?"

"Yes, I am. Sometime in January, but we're still working on the exact details. I hope you will be there."

I praised him for all the attention and coverage the Klan had received under his leadership, and he began to brag about everything he had accomplished. I knew that the key to dealing with someone like Duke, even someone like Ken, who it was clear was far from an intelligent leader, was to praise him. Suck up, offer unconditional loyalty. We spoke for about fifteen minutes, and then he said he had a KKK rally to attend in Palm Harbor that he needed to prepare for. He ended our exchange by stating he hoped to meet me when he was in town.

When I got off the phone I smiled to myself. This was going better than I ever could have planned.

Trapp and Chuck couldn't believe I was having a conversation with David Duke. "One crazy motherfucker," said Chuck.

They couldn't believe that I was doing what I was doing, and that these idiots were falling for it. They were walking around the department, telling everyone, "Can you believe what this crazy son of a bitch is doing? Talking to David Duke."

I felt that the investigation was certainly making a lot of progress. It felt good.

Anything that had to do with the Klan—from a newspaper

article, to a prank call to the department—was now sent to my attention. And it wasn't just me who was aware the Klan was trying to grow their presence in Colorado Springs. The public was also seeing these ads, reading these articles, and becoming agitated.

The first public counterprotest against the emerging KKK presence in Colorado Springs was reported to me the same day as the "Voice of the Klan" exchange with David Duke. The public outcry over the Klan presence came to my office in the form of an intelligence memo stating that blacks and Latinos were planning to commit arson against any cars belonging to KKK members, and this information was determined to be credible.

Over the next week, word began filtering throughout the public arena that David Duke was going to be in Colorado Springs in January for a "media blitz" recruitment effort on behalf of the local KKK chapter.

Uniformed Colorado Springs Police Department officers responded to a disturbance at the Southgate Shopping Center located on the south end of the city limits. They encountered eight demonstrators peacefully marching in front of stores, carrying placards with anti-KKK slogans printed in bold black letters, and handing out leaflets. One of the demonstrators I later learned was a professor at Colorado College, a prestigious local four-year private school.

The leaflet, printed in English and Spanish, was published by INCAR, the International Committee Against Racism, and it had a Denver P.O. box address. I later learned of an INCAR meeting planned for that evening and attended in an undercover capacity. This was the start of my co-undercover investigation of the Klan involving the Progressive Labor Party and its "front" organization, the International Committee Against Racism.

The group that had been protesting at the mall was no more than concerned citizens making it known that they wanted no part of a hate group like the Klan being in their town. A group like INCAR (International Committee Against Racism, sometimes referred to as just CAR, Committee Against Racism), though, posed more of a threat to groups like the Klan and law enforcement. INCAR and its parent organization, the PLP (Progressive Labor Party), were extremely radical, organized, and dedicated to their conviction of ultimately "smashing" the Ku Klux Klan. They were well planned, on message, and better able to mobilize protest demonstrations to serve their needs. They could turn violent.

It's important to remember that this was the 1970s, a period of tremendous political and civil unrest in our nation. Protest bombings in America were commonplace, especially in hard-hit cities like New York, Chicago, and San Francisco. Nearly a dozen radical underground groups, dimly remembered outfits such as the Weather Underground, the New World Liberation Front, and the Symbionese Liberation Army, set off hundreds of bombs during that tumultuous decade—so many, in fact, that many people all but accepted them as a part of daily life.

An INCAR representative from Denver, Marianne Gilbert, a Denver University professor, was present at the meeting along with a Denver representative of the Progressive Labor Party, Doug Vaughn.

Vaughn identified himself alternately as a representative of both the PLP and INCAR. INCAR was the public "front" organization of the PLP. INCAR consisted of average citizens who did not necessarily have any strong political leanings. The PLP, on the other hand, consisted of the most devout and aggressive politically engaged individuals, the bulk of whom were aligned with the Communist ideology. Doug was Communist but promoted INCAR at every opportunity. I could attend this meeting myself, as they were welcoming to blacks, and I used one of my undercover names. One Ron Stallworth in the Klan was enough, without another joining the far-leftist movements. The purpose of the meeting was to discuss the start of an INCAR chapter in Colorado Springs and to plan protest efforts against the KKK and David Duke's upcoming visit to the city.

The collective intensity of the public protest against the KKK presence quickly built to include a slew of other alphabet soup organizations: LAMECHA (Colorado College), BSU (Black Student Union—Colorado College), LaRaza (Colorado Springs), CWUC (Colorado Workers United Council—Denver), PBP (People for the Betterment of People—Colorado Springs), and ARC (Anti-Racist Coalition—Colorado Springs).

Although it was clear that the leftist factions organizing against the Klan were poorly organized, and for the most part nonviolent, I could feel the waters begin to boil in Colorado Springs, and fear and anger build. The KKK was planning burnings, marches, and recruitment. The counterforces, although far less terrorizing, could still lead to possible violence and unrest. My investigation was more important now than ever before, and little did I know that "Ron Stallworth," hopeful applicant to the KKK, would be moving up much more quickly in The Organization than anyone on my team had planned.

5

FIREMAN AND BRIMSTONE

Colorado Springs was a city of about 250,000 people, and I worked in a police department of about 250 officers. It was a typical military town, in addition to hosting the Air Force Academy and Peterson Air Force Base. It had the typical issues that come with a military town—young kids coming into town, prostitution, drugs, fights, that sort of thing. Things people get up to when they are on leave. What we didn't have were too many problems with political unrest and hate groups. One notable exception to this was Fred Wilkens, of Lakewood, Colorado, a southwestern suburb of Denver. Fred Wilkens, a firefighter for the town of Lakewood, was also the state organizer (Grand Dragon) of the Colorado Ku Klux Klan. He was a constant irritant to the Lakewood city fathers because of his racist political persuasion, which he frequently evoked in media interviews. Everything he did was within the law—just barely in some instances, but legal nonetheless. Numerous media articles reported on his extracurricular KKK activities. For example, in the February 1978 *Denver* magazine article titled "The Invisible Empire Unmasked: The KKK's Master Plan," Wilkens announced, "The Klan is the hope of the white race in Colorado and the nation, and we want to give white Americans the opportunity to join us. . . . We're going to go out into the community and let people see the new resurgent Ku Klux Klan."

Public outcry over Wilkens's position as a first responder had been registered to media outlets as well as with formal complaints to Lakewood City officials. In each instance he had been condemned publicly, rebuffed by public officials for his racial viewpoint, yet nothing could be found to officially excoriate him or his extracurricular actions, and no punishment was ever forthcoming. His stated allegiance to the Klan was deemed to be within his First Amendment rights, and as long as it did not interfere with the performance of his official duties as a Lakewood firefighter, no action could be taken against him by city officials. In fact, he apparently had an exemplary record as a firefighter including, according to one report, giving mouth-to-mouth resuscitation to a black person following a fire rescue. Wilkens was always clear to separate his professional actions from his personal convictions, and the city officials could only express their displeasure in him from a limited purview. As he clearly stated in the *Denver* magazine article, "I'm on the spot as a fireman. There are quite a few people who would like to see me lose my job. But it's my constitutional right to believe what I think is right, and I'm going to continue to the best of my ability to function as a good fireman. My job is to protect the lives and property of all citizens, white and minority groups alike. That's exactly what I will do. People ask me if I'm a racist and I tell them it depends on how you define the word. If you define it as a race hater, I definitely am not. If you define it as someone who loves his own race, then I certainly am."

But Fred loved the spotlight. He was always giving interviews, scaring up attention, and the local media seemed more than enthusiastic to profile the Klan leader firefighter. Like Duke, he wanted to mainstream the Klan, saying that "the Klan does not desire to oppose or suppress any race but believes that for each to develop to its full potential they must do so separately. Consequently, the Klan is totally opposed to racial integration and racial intermarriage . . . a total separation of the races for their mutual benefit."

Regarding blacks, Wilkens stated, "We believe they are unsuitable and unadaptable to white society. As long as they continue to participate in the white culture we will continue to have higher crime, higher taxes for welfare, lowering of educational and labor standards, and in general, a continuing deterioration of white civilization. While we wish to be on a friendly basis with black society, we choose to live totally separated. This is our feeling regarding Mexicans and other minorities as well."

So, as part of my investigation, I placed a call to Mr. Wilkens. I called Wilkens because, again, I preferred to talk to the person at the top of the food chain rather than someone—like Ken—who, being merely a local organizer, stood at the bottom of that chain and could not be specific in his replies. As an intelligence detective I wanted to know as much as possible about Wilkens and figured a phone conversation was the best way to make his acquaintance. In addition, because Lakewood was just outside of Denver, I could begin laying the groundwork for trying to get an undercover Denver officer into the Colorado KKK headquarters, since I knew that the Denver Police Intelligence Division did not have any active undercover investigation into the Klan's activities in their jurisdiction.

Wilkens answered the phone and I immediately introduced myself as a new Colorado Springs chapter Klansman.

"My name is Ron Stallworth, I'm a member of the new Colorado Springs chapter, it's a pleasure, Mr. Wilkens."

He was very warm, and glad to hear from me.

He and David Duke loved to be fawned over—all you had to do was appeal to their sense of self-worth. Admire them.

"I want to learn as much as I can about The Cause," I said. I requested any literature that would help me improve my knowledge of the history and ways of the Klan. He promised to send me several issues of *The Crusader,* the Klan newspaper. I also asked about my membership card, and he said he would check into its status. He knew it had not been approved as of this date but told me if I did not receive it within the next two days to get back to him and he would personally contact the national headquarters in Louisiana to push through the process.

I once again asked about the alleged impending Colorado Springs visit of David Duke in January. Wilkens confirmed Duke's arrival as tentatively around the first week of January. He hoped to have a hundred robed Klansmen for the proposed march. He asked about a recent *Gazette Telegraph* newspaper interview given by local organizer Ken O'dell. He wanted to know my personal reaction to the interview. I told him Ken expressed the goals and objectives of The Organization very well, and I thought it would be well received by the public. Wilkens asked if he should give more personal interviews to the media in Colorado Springs. I told him yes, without offering specific reasons, and he immediately expressed a desire to meet me in Lakewood to discuss organizing efforts for the Colorado Springs area. I, of course, agreed.

Wilkens explained, "The hub of the Klan plan revolves around political activity." The goal was to get Klansmen elected to political offices at all levels of government throughout Colorado. If they could not find qualified Klansmen to run for elective office, Wilkens said, "We will also support non-Klansmen who share our philosophy. If a candidate wants our public endorsement we'll give it to him or we may support him with financial aid. The important thing is to get the right kind of thinking into government." He mentioned how well the "niggers" organized themselves politically, and that we needed to do the same to protect what we had.

"I have to go, but I look forward to meeting you, Ron." I thanked him for his time (always being a suck-up) and we then ended our call.

Eight days later Ken called my undercover alter ego Chuck, thinking he was talking to me, on the undercover telephone line in the Narcotics office to explain the status of my membership card. He told Chuck the card had not yet arrived and I was therefore still prevented from full participation in Klan activities. He said he personally spoke with "Mr. Duke" yesterday and was told he would be in Colorado Springs on January 1.

Since the last meeting with Chuck at the Corner Pocket Lounge, Ken had taken a trip home to San Antonio, Texas. After his return, he revealed, there had been several requests for media interviews, which he would be following up on. He added there were a hundred Klan applicants in the Colorado Springs chapter, but it was almost impossible to get them robed in time for the proposed January march. Ken did say he was not ready to totally give up on the idea of the march, but at this point it was not looking good; apparently it took about a month after members applied before they received their robes and could proudly display their public personae as Klansmen. He expressed a desire to meet directly with me (Chuck) in the near future, and the conversation ended.

A half hour later, Ken again called the narcotics undercover telephone line and asked to speak to "Ron." Chuck was not in the office at the time, so another one of the narcotics detectives, pretending to be him (me), spoke with Ken, who told him that he had just learned from the Klan National Headquarters that my membership had been approved. The detective was assured that my membership card should be arriving in the mail in the next couple of days.

On the twenty-eighth of November I learned that the local KKK chapter had an account at the Bank of Fountain Valley, located on State Highway 85-87 in the Security area near Fort Carson. The account, in the names of Ken O'dell and Jennifer L. Strong (I would later learn she was connected with the Klan), was also listed as a corporation in the name of the White Peoples Organization. The initial deposit was $44.00.

Later that same day, I telephoned Fred Wilkens in Lakewood, Colorado. He told me he had recently returned from the national Klan convention in New Orleans and that David Duke confirmed he would be arriving in Denver on January 6, 1979. Wilkens said there would probably be a planned march in Colorado Springs on either January 7 or 8 in honor of the Grand Wizard. He explained that the uncertainty was based on a large portion of the state's membership not owning white Klan robes, and because they wanted significant media coverage it was imperative that Klan marchers be seen by the public in the symbolic context of their white robes.

Ken and Fred were obsessed with the idea of us being in full robed force, and I think it's important to take a look at the origin of these robes, which instantly conjure feelings of terror and hate in the minds of any decent American, and where they came from.

From its 1869 origin in Pulaski, Tennessee, the Ku Klux Klan and its Confederate soldier membership under the leadership of the first recognized Grand Wizard, General Nathan Bedford Forrest, wore white sheets with holes cut out to expose the mouth, nose, and eyes, though some just exposed the eyes. According to historical records, some even placed robes on their horses. To what purpose was this ruse being played?

Recently freed slaves were known by their slave masters and the general white populace to hold strong superstitious beliefs in ghosts and otherworldly spirits. These beliefs were especially strong in reference to recently deceased Confederate soldiers. Taking advantage of these superstitions, the original Klansmen sought to capitalize on this "otherworldly" belief by terrorizing the slaves into believing the white-sheeted horses and riders were the ghostly spirits of those fallen Confederate soldiers and their steeds, returned to earthly form to ensure that the ways and traditions of the antebellum South were properly observed and maintained by the freed men and women. The success of the early Klansmen in accomplishing this objective would, in effect, negate the results of the recently fought war and the government's attempt at Reconstruction of the physically and morally battered South.

Another symbolic representation was the "fiery cross" burned at the site of those—white and black—who had offended them. One can only imagine the state of mind of those superstitious slaves at the sight of a "ghostly apparition" of horses and riders and the "demonic" spectacle of the fiery cross as vengeful action for alleged sins against the honored traditions of the "Old South."

Traditionally, the burning of a cross, or a "cross-lighting ceremony," is considered a religious celebration. The burning of a religious symbol has never been seen by Klan members as a sign of desecration; it has always been considered an honorable representation of their Christian faith and beliefs. But they historically used it to strike terror in those who feared the force and wrath of the Klan. In other words, from its very beginning the Ku Klux Klan and its members were dedicated to the cause of domestic terrorism.

Though such superstitious beliefs no longer persist, the symbols are still used to induce terror in the hearts and minds of the Klan's victims.

The notion of a hundred white-robed Klansmen marching in formation reported on by heavy media scrutiny would do just that—incite terror in the citizens, especially the black citizens of Colorado Springs and their young children, unaccustomed to such terrible actions.

Wilkens mentioned that while in New Orleans he personally led the march because David Duke had received death threats from members of the Progressive Labor Party. He said Duke refused to back down from their intimidating efforts and the march proceeded without incident.

Wilkens said he received a lot of negative response from the "nigger" population, but the security provided by the New Orleans police was excellent, and to avoid a confrontation with the "niggers" the Klan had cooperated with the police and conducted the march one hour before its regularly scheduled time.

By the time the "niggers" gathered for their staged protest, the march was completed. He explained that two Klansmen had been arrested because they were carrying guns and fired a couple of rounds into the air to "frighten the niggers."

"Do you know what that idiot O'dell told the press?" Wilkens asked. I had seen that Ken had promised a hundred robed Klansmen to be present for David Duke's march in January. As a result, Wilkens stated he now felt obligated as the Colorado state organizer to ensure the success of Ken's statement; a large number of members without robes would leave a bad impression on the Klan with the news media. Wilkens added that he would really like to meet with me to further discuss organizing strategy in the Colorado Springs area. Wilkens asked me to be his Colorado Springs media conduit and arrange interviews for David Duke's time in the city. I told him I would be honored to do so.

Wilkens told me to expect a package from him—sent to the undercover P.O. box—containing his copy of the Klan bylaws so that I "could learn to properly conduct myself in the ways of the Klan." He added that my membership card should also arrive in the mail within the next week.

I asked Wilkens if he knew of any black extremist group that planned on disrupting the proposed January march. He said no, he had not heard of any particular group planning to disrupt the march, but the Klan was prepared to deal with any situation with a counterdemonstration. He added that in the event of such action he hoped it would be nonviolent; however, if violence did erupt and was directed at any Klansman, they would take appropriate measures, on which he would not elaborate.

In the interim, as I conducted follow-up on the various names and information that had thus far been accumulated, the anti-Klan protest movement started to pick up steam. One example was reported in a newspaper article that appeared in the now defunct *Colorado Springs Sun* (November 29, 1978).

In the article, the Committee Against Racism (CAR) and the People for the Betterment of People announced they were changing their scheduled December 21 protest march against the Klan to December 16. This came following a meeting of local civil rights advocates that was attended by about sixty people and based on complaints from Colorado College students that the original date was too close to their Christmas break and a one-week pushback would better accommodate their ability to generate a large student turnout.

The primary reason for the meeting, however, was to discuss tactics aimed at uniting community opposition to the Klan. The sixty-person attendance was notable because the meeting was not publicized but rather the result of word-of-mouth notification over a short time. The most disturbing aspect of this tactical discussion was offered by Doug Vaughn of the Denver Chapter of the International Committee Against Racism (INCAR). Vaughn proclaimed membership in both INCAR and the PLP. Circumstances determined which one he claimed at a given time. The difference between the two was that INCAR was for the general public and PLP members tended to be staunch, devoted Communists. Doug called for a violent confrontation with the Klan: "When racist vermin like the Klan and Nazis wriggle out from under a rock, we believe in smashing the rock right back down on them."

There was a third tactical position offered in response to the Klan's January march. The Colorado College Black Student

Union's position was to completely ignore them. Their spokes-person felt this would show the Klan that they lacked the pub-lic's support. "People watching at home on TV will think one of two things. They'll either think that people are scared or that they don't give a damn. Neither are very positive reactions."

After much discussion, the group came to the conclusion that the Klan was (1) clever, (2) opportunistic, and (3) violent, and could act at any time. They felt they had to make appropriate preparations to counter any immediate efforts on the part of the Ku Klux Klan to gain a strong foothold in and against the people of Colorado Springs. They eventually decided that the best reaction to a Klan march would probably be to have a small group pass out anti-Klan leaflets and hold signs to let the pub-lic know the Klan was being opposed and to inform them of the Klan's real purpose. I attended the meeting in an undercover capacity.

The anti-Klan meetings were attended primarily by college students, a few professionals, college instructors, and concerned citizens. They were housewives and people from all walks of life concerned about the Klan having a viable presence in the city. They were not well organized, and they didn't have any plans of attack. It was clear they were unable to unify—they had so many different groups and agendas that they couldn't come to-gether.

This meeting demonstrated the wide range of visceral atti-tudes toward the emerging presence of the Klan and the lack of consensus as to the best means of addressing their presence; from a march, to a violent confrontation, to completely disregarding their presence, before finally settling on passing out leaflets and holding signs with anti-Klan slogans. The state of mind of those

professing deep concern for having the Klan in their midst varied significantly.

On December 1, a significant development occurred in the
relationship between Ken O'dell and me. He called Chuck to
announce a Klan meeting at his home and explained there were
two purposes for the meeting: (1) Butch and his wife would be
leaving the area, returning to their home base of California, and
(2) he (Ken) was leaving the Army, and returning to his home
in San Antonio, Texas, sometime in January 1979. As a result,
the Klan would need a new local organizer. Ken told Chuck that
he had been impressed with me throughout our various talks
and thought I (Chuck) "would make a great local organizer."

Of course both Chuck and I were caught completely off
guard by this very unique development. In my phone conversations with Ken there had never been any indication that he was
even remotely thinking about moving in this direction. Had I
known that he was considering such a move I, of course, would
have sat down with my sergeant and Chuck and tried to plot
some kind of strategic response to his declaration of "Ron Stallworth" assuming the leadership role of the Colorado Springs
chapter of the Knights of the Ku Klux Klan. The greatest impediment to this whole possibility was the issue of "entrapment,"
and Chuck, like the excellent undercover investigator he was,
immediately grasped this and put it in perspective in his follow-
up response.

Thinking about the legal issue of "entrapment," Chuck tried
to redirect Ken's thinking on the subject by telling him he did
not know if any of the other members would receive his idea
with the same sense of enthusiasm.

As undercover officers we were always thinking of how to

avoid entrapment, which is willfully deceiving a target into wrong-doing. So, for example, we couldn't organize a cross burning and then arrest the Klan participants for conspiring to terrorize Colorado Springs. So a leadership position obviously presented not only more challenges, but also tremendous possible rewards.

As undercover investigators, police can legitimately use various forms of deception to gain information or apprehend a suspect, but they cannot persuade an innocent person to commit a crime he or she was not predisposed to commit, nor can they coerce a suspect into doing so even if they are certain she or he is a criminal. Every undercover investigator must keep the issue of entrapment at the forefront of his or her mind during the course of an investigation, as it will become the cornerstone of any defense effort once an arrest has been made. One slip can mean the difference between a failed or successful investigation and subsequent prosecution or dismissal.

Whenever I (or Chuck) talked to Klan members, we had to be careful not to steer the conversation into territory that might persuade one of them to do something they normally would not conceive of doing. This was often difficult because many times they asked for my (our) opinion on what steps or direction they should take in carrying out some plan of action that often put them on a path of conflict with either the public or, more directly, the police. It would have been quite easy for me (or Chuck) to manipulate conversations that would have guaranteed they would commit criminal acts, thus allowing for their arrest and prosecution. Instead, we steered (or tried to) such conversations away from acts of conflict, which proved beneficial to our objective of intelligence gathering and still provided for the public safety and welfare. The rule of law governing entrapment always kept us in check and also prevented us from crossing the line into committing criminal acts ourselves.

Ken continued to press Chuck to attend the meeting at his house that evening and for him to consider replacing him in the role of local organizer. Chuck declined the invitation because of a prior commitment and also told Ken he preferred to remain a "silent" member of the Klan, one whose identity is kept in the shadows, rather than assume the more public role of local organizer. His justification for this preference was his job working for the Public Works Department within the Colorado Springs city government. We often used city government jobs as cover occupations when conducting an investigation. It was an effective cover because city government is a huge operation with thousands of employees.

Ken claimed to have spoken with David Duke the day before and said he would be arriving in Colorado Springs on January 6 for a five-day visit. If they met the hundred-robed-member number by January while Duke was in the city, the march would go on as scheduled.

On December 5, Chuck telephoned Ken and was told there would be another meeting at his home in three days to further discuss replacing chapter officers. Chuck agreed to be there. On December 8, Chuck, in his guise as Ron Stallworth, arrived at Ken O'dell's house and was greeted by his wife, Anita. She proved to be an anomaly in the Ken O'dell-KKK relationship because of her ethnic background. One of the minority groups targeted by the Klan are Mexican-Americans, especially if a chapter is dominant in a section of the country heavily populated by that particular group. The Klan will always, however, have at the top of their racist agenda blacks and Jews. In the case of Ken O'dell's wife, the two of them were from San Antonio, Texas, and she was of Mexican heritage. Chuck made the decision, rightly, not to comment on this upon entering the gathering.

Ken had proven himself to be less than believable in our interactions. He was constantly inventing facts to make himself seem more important than he was, pulling member numbers out of thin air and bragging about plans he had no way of seeing to fruition. As frustrating and unreliable as he was, he was still a tremendous asset and entry into the world of the Klan.

There were seven people present at Ken's house (including O'dell and his wife) who were all later determined to be soldiers at Fort Carson. One of these was a Joe Stewart, who was to prove to be a pivotal member of the Klan chapter. He was introduced to Chuck as Ken's "second in command." "Tim" was introduced as the Klan's treasurer and "Bob" as the "Nighthawk" (bodyguard). This was the first full revelation of the Klan chapter's leadership structure. Ken explained that the meeting had four items of discussion:

1. Possible lawsuit against the *Gazette Telegraph* newspaper
2. Introduction of the KKK into the Colorado State Penitentiary
3. Recruitment of new members
4. Election of a new local organizer

Their lawsuit was based on a Klan advertisement the newspaper allegedly agreed to run for a certain number of days and suddenly reneged. Ken stated Fred Wilkens and the Denver organization supported the filing of the lawsuit, and they were enthusiastic about moving forward. Ken then moved on to the issue of the Klan in the penitentiary. The white prison population was a group to target for recruitment. Ken pointed out that they were locked up and treated the same as black and Latino criminals. They needed to know they had brothers on the outside looking out for them, and a community on the inside that they could rely on. Chuck was told that only one inmate had ever received Klan literature before. He did not offer any details as to why there had been only one, and whether he was still in prison, whether he still received Klan literature, or if it had been intercepted by prison authorities.

Ken's plan was to begin sending copies of *The Crusader* newspaper, along with membership applications to join the Klan, to white inmates. He made it clear that there would be an active attempt at organizing a Klan "den" (chapter) inside the Colorado State Penitentiary at Canon City, Colorado.

"In addition to reaching out to the men in Colorado State, I also want to talk about recruitment strategy," said Ken. "Now, we need a hundred members for Mr. Duke's visit in January. In order to do this I'm putting forth a new policy. Each of you needs to recruit three new members. And in turn those three members will recruit three members and so on and so on. That way we will grow exponentially." I could imagine over the wire the smug grin on Ken's face as he mispronounced "exponentially." But I also thought that this presented an opportunity to expand my investigation. By having Chuck bring in at least another officer I could double my manpower.

Ken then brought up the issue of election of a new local organizer. He felt there was an immediate need to have someone who was nonmilitary take over the reins of leadership. That type of person would be the best representative for the Klan because he would not be hampered by military regulations or time frames regarding duty assignments, discharge, etc.

Without further fanfare, Ken announced to those assembled he had chosen Ron Stallworth (Chuck) as his choice to be the new local organizer. As justification for his decision, Ken explained that I (Chuck) had proven myself "to be a loyal and dedicated Klansman." He then asked the others for input, and they unanimously affirmed their support of his decision.

Personally, I felt this was excellent for the investigation if "Ron" was to be made Klan organizer. Riskier, yes, but also so much potential reward. We could pull it off, I knew, if we just worked closely with the district attorney every step of the way. By being in a position of semi-leadership, we would have so much more knowledge and information at our disposal.

Chuck, to his immense credit in the moment, was again conscious of entrapment and the ramifications of being in such a high position of responsibility and how that could affect the direction and possible outcome of this investigation if it reached an ultimate conclusion of multiple criminal charges and arrests. He thanked Ken and the others for the "high honor" but stated he was not certain he could devote the necessary time required to fulfill the duties of the local organizer. Ken brushed that off and expressed confidence in my (Chuck's) ability to arrange my schedule to accommodate the necessary duties of the local organizer. Nothing further was mentioned about the subject for the rest of the evening, though the matter was far from put to rest.

Several times during the meeting, Ken commented on the subject of violence. Officially, they had taken a page out of the playbook of Martin Luther King Jr., actually. Nonviolent action and organization in fact had changed American culture. But Ken walked a different walk, it was clear. While listening to the evening's discussion over Chuck's wireless body transmitter (I was always in one of the surveillance vehicles during these face-to-face meetings) and in later discussions with him following the meeting, we concluded that Ken supported any type of violence against those who were not members of the Klan, despite previous statements of a nonviolent credo.

Ken wanted to organize a group to go to El Paso for a "border watch." This would mean staking out the border in their cars and trucks with rifles with scopes and shooting anyone they saw trying to cross the Rio Grande. A Klan armed watch along the Rio Grande border of Mexico was in keeping with David Duke's approach to immigration control.

After the meeting Ken proudly showed Chuck his arsenal of thirteen rifles and shotguns and one cap and ball pistol along with his equipment for reloading ammunition. He commented that he had additional weapons in every room in his house and that he also carried weapons in each of his vehicles. This was valuable information to know in the event we ever had to execute a search warrant at his residence or attempt to arrest him while he was in transit.

Just prior to Chuck's departure, Ken showed him a piece of paper with approximately twenty-five names that he said represented the membership of the local chapter—"Everyone you'll be leader of," he said. He reiterated that if each one brought in three recruits the organization would grow substantially. Unfortunately Ken just showed the list to Chuck, who wasn't able to memorize it. But it was clear that membership, no matter how loose this devilish brotherhood might be, was larger than we had thought.

Ken walked Chuck to the door, shook his hand, and stressed again what a fine organizer he would make. Chuck thanked him and left. In the car outside I breathed a sigh of relief that the meeting was over and began the drive back to the police station, knowing that the Klan in my city was more powerful than I had known, but also excited that my investigation was certainly going to expand.

6

PART OF OUR POSSE

Following the meeting at Ken's house, I immediately put in a request with Sergeant Trapp to expand my undercover team. We needed Chuck to bring in at least one new member. Trapp was, as always, fully supportive of my investigation and immediately went to the chief to clear another undercover officer to join my team. Arthur was, as expected, not happy about this, but he had no say in the matter. I did not report to him, and he could not interfere with my investigation. I chose Jimmy to go undercover with Chuck. It made the most sense, as he was already helping me with the surveillance missions. Now with a new "recruit" I was ready to dig even deeper into the Klan.

On December 11 I paid a visit to Guy Thomas, an investigator with the Intelligence Unit at the Colorado State Penitentiary in Canon City, Colorado. I wanted to discuss Ken's plans to expand Klan membership within the prison. I alerted him to the fact that the Klan would be attempting to recruit inmates via Klan literature mailings. Thomas informed me that a Klan newspaper, *The Crusader*, had been confiscated from an inmate originally from Weld County, the northern area of the state bordering Wyoming and home of the University of Northern Colorado in Greeley. This inmate, according to Investigator Thomas, was now claiming Klan membership and had recruited a fellow inmate. A third inmate was receiving the newspaper directly from Klan headquarters in Metairie, Louisiana. A fourth inmate had been receiving letters from a member of the National Socialist White People's Party (NSWPP) out of Arlington, Virginia. Investigator Thomas promised to keep me informed of any further developments inside the prison system.

That same day Chuck received a telephone call from Ken telling him he had good news to report. Two days earlier he had received a call from members of the local Posse Comitatus expressing a desire to work cooperatively with the Ku Klux Klan. This was a potential major development because the Posse Comitatus was, at that time, one of the most significant right-wing ideological extremist groups in Colorado.

The term *"Posse Comitatus"* is Latin meaning "force of the county." As a loosely organized far right social movement it was opposed to the federal government, preferring "localism," or that there was no legitimate form of government above that of the county level, with the sheriff being the highest form of legal authority. If, in their belief, the sheriff refuses to carry out the will of the citizens, "he shall be removed by the Posse to the most populated intersection of streets in the township and at high noon be hung by the neck until sundown as an example to those who would subvert the law."

Some Posse members were practicing survivalists and were active in the formation of the armed citizen militias of the 1990s. Like the Ku Klux Klan, they embraced anti-Semitic and white supremacist beliefs that the federal government is under the control of ZOG (Zionist Occupied Government), part of a Jewish conspiracy.

One of the tactics pioneered by the Posse in the 1970s and used quite frequently in Colorado Springs to terrorize law enforcement and other government officials was the use of false liens filed against property and other forms of paper terrorism. These liens would tie the victims up in court for extended periods of time and force them to spend money and other resources on attorney fees to defend what was legally theirs. I personally knew of some officers who attempted to sell their houses only to find out at a certain point in the process that they could not do so because of a Posse lien placed against it.

As a uniformed officer, I occasionally encountered Posse members during routine traffic stops. Because I was a city police officer and not a sheriff's deputy, they refused to recognize my authority and openly challenged my right to stop them, much less talk to them. The fact that I was black did not sit kindly with them because, like the Klan, they took a dim view of anyone who did not have white skin. They challenged our actions in court under the misguided belief that our authority was not sanctioned by the U.S. Constitution, and they always lost. Our Intelligence Unit continuously monitored the Posse and its membership but we had never been able to initiate an undercover investigation on their group in the manner similar to that of the KKK.

Ken's announcement of a possible merger of the two groups was therefore a significant turn of events in the investigation and held great interest not only for me personally but also for my sergeant. The question was how could we in our current circumstance exploit this situation to our advantage and expand the scope of the investigation. The Posse Comitatus was a big pain in the ass for the cops at that time, and Ken's wanting to merge with the PC created a unique set of problems. It was to our advantage to have both of these groups be separate, as their joining together would only strengthen them, but with the merger also came the opportunity for information. We would be able to identify the members, and our investigation would only widen. The PC was larger than the Klan in Colorado, and its members were, to put it bluntly, nuts. They would openly carry guns on the streets, into stores, everywhere. They were unloaded, in accordance with the law, but as a police officer how are you supposed to know if a gun openly carried is loaded or not? They were, on the whole, angry, dangerous men.

Ken told Chuck he was impressed with the viewpoints of the Posse. He stated that on the previous day he had hosted some Posse members at his home, and they, in turn, had invited him to attend a meeting they had scheduled for tomorrow, December 12. Ken added that he was allowed to take two additional Klan representatives with him, and Bob, the Klan treasurer, would definitely be one of them. He said he was considering the second representative from among Bob the bodyguard, Joe his second in command, and me, Ron Stallworth, and would let them know soon.

Ken was hoping Fred Wilkens would be able to attend the Posse meeting because he wanted to show the film *The Birth of a Nation*, but Wilkens was not able to be there, so that idea was canceled. He suggested a second special meeting with the Posse

the following week, on December 19, for the showing of the film
with Wilkens present. The importance of *The Birth of a Nation*
in relationship to the modern Ku Klux Klan cannot be overstated.

Based on a novel by Thomas Dixon Jr., a North Carolina
minister, the movie was released in 1915 by acclaimed director
D. W. Griffith. In the early film age of short, silent slapstick
comedies, *The Birth of a Nation* was a two-hour-and-forty-five-
minute panoramic epic that set film industry standards for its
time. Until the 1960s, it was cited as the greatest American film
according to the late movie critic Roger Ebert in a review of the
film and its impact. In fact for many years in the early twenti-
eth century, *The Birth of a Nation* was considered the most
popular film ever made and thought to express the widespread,
generally acceptable views of white Americans. In Ebert's
2003 review of the film, he quotes the female star of the movie,
Lillian Gish, acknowledging Griffith's paternalistic reply to ac-
cusations that he was anti-Negro: "To say that is like saying I
am against children, as they were our children, whom we loved
and cared for all of our lives." Griffith was an unapologetic white
southerner of the nineteenth century whose movie reflected the
attitudes of his peers who were unable to see black Americans
as fellow beings worthy of rights.

The Birth of a Nation told a Klan version of history, a narrative of the legend of the Klan as the savior of the South during
Reconstruction. The film plays on the heroics of the great Civil
War battles, the stereotypes of blacks as sex-crazed rapists and
loyal servants to their white masters, the myths of Reconstruction, the northern congressmen who wanted to punish the
South for the war, the carpetbaggers (northerners in the South

after the war who were seeking private gain under the government's Reconstruction program), and power-mad black Reconstruction legislators and soldiers.

The movie tells a love story between a southern colonel and the nurse who tended him. As the suspense builds, the sister of the colonel leaps to her death to avoid being raped by a "lecherous black." Appalled by this outrage, the Ku Klux Klan enters the picture to rid the land of the scourge that has descended upon it. To pave the way for the widespread acceptance of the movie, Thomas Dixon, an old classmate of President Woodrow Wilson, arranged a private screening for him, his cabinet, and their families. It was reported that the president emerged from the screening very moved by the film, declaring it "like writing history with lightning . . . my only regret is that it is all so terribly true."

The movie went on to gross $18 million ($409 million in 2013 dollars). Its impact was so powerful that it has often been credited with setting the stage for the Klan revival of 1915.

William J. Simmons, the man who took the title of Grand Wizard and initiated the revival, recognized the propaganda value of *The Birth of a Nation* to the Klan and used it as a promotional tool to win recruits to the organization. Modern Klan leaders, including Ken, Wilkens, and Simmons's successor as Grand Wizard, David Duke, still used the movie as a recruiting gimmick and provided their own personal narrative to their audience to rally them to the cause.

Ken told Chuck that an associate of the Posse Comitatus possessed an original KKK saber and belt buckle belonging to the first Grand Wizard, General Nathan Bedford Forrest, and he wanted to buy them. He added that another good reason for combining forces with the Posse was that they offered a course for sixty-five dollars on how to avoid paying income taxes. He insisted that the income tax was unconstitutional, and the course offered the forms and taught the correct way to fill them out to protest paying any type of taxes. If the two groups joined forces, Ken stated, he was going to recommend all Klan members take the course.

At this point in the conversation Ken began to press Chuck on the fact that he was, thus far, the only Klan member who had not recommended a person for new membership. Ken was lying, no one else was bringing in three members either, but his insistence on Chuck, or I should say "Ron," bringing in new members and becoming an organizer was beginning to present a real problem. There are only so many times you can say "I'm trying" before people like Ken become angry, or worse, suspicious.

After Chuck indicated he would attempt to talk a friend into coming for an interview, Ken said if Chuck wished to remain a "silent" member then he would conduct the interview as if Chuck were a new recruit himself. Meaning that Ken would make Chuck pretend to be a first-time recruit alongside whomever he brought.

December 11 proved to be a very productive informational day in the barely monthlong investigation. It also proved to be the start of a slight change of direction in the scope of the investigation because I was personally contacted by an Air Force sergeant assigned to NORAD (North American Aerospace Defense Command). NORAD is a joint American and Canadian military mission charged with the aerospace warning, control, sovereignty, and defense of the North American continent. The mission "includes the monitoring of man-made objects in space,

and the detection, validation, and warning of attack against North America whether by aircraft, missiles, or space vehicles, through mutual support arrangements with other commands." It was established in 1958, an effect of the cold war with the former Soviet Union, with the main technical facility located inside Cheyenne Mountain on the west side of Interstate 25 across from Fort Carson. It is considered a "Top Security Clearance" facility.

I was contacted by NORAD because news of a black cop running an undercover investigation into the KKK had begun to make the rounds among the law enforcement community. For example, I was testifying on an old drug case when, during a break in the action between attorneys, the judge covered the microphone, leaned over to me, and asked how my KKK investigation was coming along. When I asked him how he knew about that, he said that everyone was talking about it. On another occasion I went into the local "cop bar," across the street from the courthouse, where criminal justice officials congregated after work, and would occasionally be greeted with a request to see my KKK membership card, which I carried in my wallet. Someone would inevitably buy me a drink and offer a toast on my behalf loud enough for anyone nearby to hear: "To the only black man crazy enough to join the KKK." Glasses would be raised in my direction and then someone would say, "Show us your KKK card."

This knowledge was even more widespread within the police department. We were approximately 250 sworn officers, second only to the Denver Police Department; with civilian support personnel our total complement of employees was perhaps just over 300. In many respects we were like a small rural town where everyone knows everyone and their personal secrets are not too personal.

I found myself fielding more and more questions from various officers who wanted an avenue to somehow insert themselves into the investigation. Some of these officers were seeking a path into the Intelligence Unit and thought they could ingratiate themselves by doing something consequential concerning the investigation; by currying favor with me they could also make me an ally in their quest to be assigned to the unit. Others wanted to be a part of what was unique criminal justice system scuttlebutt and wanted their names attached to it. I wasn't exactly thrilled about the gossip, but I can't say I wasn't proud of my work, and a little praise here or there feels good.

The NORAD sergeant introduced himself and immediately let me know he was also a black man. He told me he had lived in several cities during his lifetime: Indianapolis, Chicago, St. Louis, and Petersburg, Virginia, and had witnessed Klan activity in a couple of them during the 1960s. He was fully aware of what the Klan was capable of doing to destroy a community and damage the people living there and wanted to do what he could to prevent them from doing the same in Colorado Springs.

Prior to joining the Air Force eighteen years before (1960) he had at different times been a "card-carrying" member of both the Black Muslims and the Black Panther Party, and he was still in touch with members of both groups. Approximately ten days earlier he received a phone call from a Muslim member in Chicago, an associate of Louis Farrakhan, who wanted to know about the "atmosphere" in Colorado Springs since the emergence of the Klan.

The sergeant indicated the Muslim member wanted to know

if the black citizens of Colorado Springs would support a counter-demonstration led by a small group of Chicago Muslims against the Klan and if any "machinery" (weapons) would be needed.

The sergeant claimed he told both groups the Colorado Springs atmosphere was not ready for such activity and suggested they not come to the city. He felt the Black Panthers would take his advice; however, he believed the Muslims were prepared to arrive about the same time as David Duke. He added that if the Muslims did not demonstrate against Duke they would probably attempt to open a mosque in Colorado Springs. He offered to cooperate with my investigation by introducing me to any Panthers or Muslims who might appear in the city. These forces might have been countering a white supremacist hate group, but they also presented their own problems for me as a law enforcement officer—violence, drugs.

I thanked the sergeant for the call, told him it would not be helpful to have these forces in Colorado Springs, and that it was in the best interest of not only him, but also the city for them to stay where they are. They were going to be, for lack of a better term, outside agitators.

On December 12 I received a report from uniformed patrol officers of the Colorado Springs Police Department regarding Michael W. Miller, a Fort Carson soldier. The officers had responded to a disturbance complaint at The Bunny Club, a popular bar frequented by military personnel. Miller, following an argument with bar personnel regarding an allegation of being shortchanged, began cursing at the bar owner. He pulled out a "business card" from his wallet and threw it on the bar and said, "I should firebomb this place. I've done it before."

The card bore the printed logo of the Knights of the Ku Klux Klan with the address and phone number of the national headquarters in Metairie, Louisiana, and the slogan "Racial Purity Is America's Security," which became Duke's campaign slogan for his first run at the Louisiana State Senate. Stamped on the left side of the front of the card was the name White People Org, the same name as the corporation listed on the bank account for the KKK in Ken O'dell's name. The card also bore P.O. Box 4771, the same P.O. box number listed in the newspaper ad I responded to back in October.

When confronted by officers, Miller first denied putting the card on the bar, then later said it wasn't a crime to carry KKK cards and pass them out. He also showed officers a card (#3860) issued by the State of Oregon that authorized him to buy explosives. He told officers he was trained in explosives by the U.S. Army. Officers determined he was clearly intoxicated and removed him from the bar and turned him over to military authorities.

As a follow-up to this incident I contacted Fort Carson Military Police/CID (Criminal Investigation Detachment) officials and learned that Miller was a known alcoholic whose job was reconnaissance, and he was, in fact, trained in the use of explosives.

Miller's first sergeant—a black man—said he was aware of his KKK involvement, as Miller had flaunted that fact to him on several occasions. In fact, the sergeant said Miller had previously issued an implied threat to him by saying he had polished a

.30-06 caliber round of ammunition engraved with his name and intended to present it to him as a gift one day.

When I asked what the sergeant had done to discipline Miller for this obvious breach of conduct, the military authorities stated nothing. The sergeant apparently just laughed it off as "Miller being Miller." His alcoholism continued, his KKK involvement continued, and his implied threats to the sergeant's life continued. Miller continued being himself, which, in the eyes of his first sergeant—a black man—was apparently "normal." The military officials were apathetic and just accepted the fact that this man—this soldier representing the government and people of the United States—was an avowed racist and member of the Ku Klux Klan.

Later that same day I telephoned David Duke at his Louisiana headquarters regarding the status of my Ku Klux Klan membership card. Duke answered the phone and I introduced myself as Ron Stallworth, one of the new Colorado Springs chapter members that had spoken to him earlier.

"Oh, yes. Hi, how are you?" he asked. David Duke was always quite cordial, excited even to speak with a strange, fresh recruit. I told him it had been nearly two months since I mailed my membership application to the national headquarters and I still had not received my card. I was eager to get the card because I could not fully participate in any Klan activities until my membership had been officially processed and I held the card in my hand. I was desperate to get involved in the ongoing efforts to reclaim the white race from the media dominance of the niggers and Jews, but because of Klan rules I was restricted from that participation. I expressed to "Mr. Duke" my frustration and asked if he could do anything to resolve the issue.

He told me to wait a minute and I heard the distinct sound of papers being shuffled in the background. After a few minutes or so he located my application with the membership fee attached. He apologized for the processing delay, stating there had been some administrative problems of late in the office and they had gotten backlogged.

"I promise to personally process your application, Mr. Stallworth," he said, and to "get it in the mail to you as soon as possible." I thanked him profusely and terminated the conversation.

It was hard to keep a straight face while speaking with David, if I'm being honest. It was also very hard to keep my real opinions to myself. When I was confronted with this blatant racism it honestly came off as silly. Just nonsense.

Sergeant Trapp would listen in on my calls to Ken, David, or Fred Wilkens, and start laughing, running out of the room because he would be overheard on the phone.

In a darkly funny way, we actually were having fun.

On December 13 Ken phoned Chuck to update him on the Posse Comitatus. The originally scheduled meeting had been postponed until later that day and confirmed that Fred Wilkens would attend the meeting and *The Birth of a Nation* would be shown. Chuck agreed to attend after Ken told him he had to meet the sheriff regarding an incident he'd had with a "nigger kid." Apparently he'd had an altercation with a black teenager in his neighborhood, and he wanted to plot some sort of retaliation with Fred, something I could never confirm.

Chuck told Ken about a friend of his who was interested in joining the Klan. Ken had been pressing all of the members to recruit three new members but had particularly stressed to Chuck that he had not brought forth any potential prospects, and he perked up at this bit of news. He said he looked forward to meeting Chuck's friend and interviewing him for membership. They agreed to meet at seven o'clock that evening at the Corner Pocket Lounge.

At 7:00 P.M., Chuck and CSPD Narcotics Detective James (Jimmy) W. Rose met with Ken at appointed time and place. I was in my usual spot in the car outside. With Ken were Bob the bodyguard and Tim the treasurer. While Ken sat at a table with Jim, explaining the Klan, Bob, clearly trying to separate Chuck from Jim and Ken's conversation, asked Chuck to shoot some pool with him.

During their game, Bob told Chuck that all of the soldiers he met at Ken's house on December 8 had only been members of the Klan since the first of November. He said the local chapter had approximately twenty-four members and most of them were military personnel. He also indicated that the membership were in full support of Ken's selection of him (me) as his replacement as local organizer.

Chuck again tried to deflect this subject by telling Bob he was not interested in the position. A short time later Tim also joined the conversation about the local organizer position. He too felt that Chuck was the appropriate person for the job "due to his position in the community."

We had made such a positive impression on Ken because both and Chuck and I had just spewed the most disgusting hate from that first phone call on, and then reinforced those feelings. As undercover investigators we would never have challenged Ken, who was—I can't stress this enough—a total idiot. We stroked his ego, made him feel like a great leader. He would never be suspicious of someone who thought he was doing a great job. This was necessary for the success of the investigation.

Tim said that when he discharged from the Army he would return to Boston to set up his own Klan "den" (chapter).

While Bob and Tim were busy with Chuck, Jim was busy having a discussion with Ken and a white female named Carole who had shown up to meet Ken about joining the Klan. She was an independent truck driver who claimed her reason for wanting membership was that eleven years ago she had been assaulted by members of the Black Panther Party. She told Jim and Ken that because of that incident she had been illegally carrying a firearm all those years—in the boot she was wearing—and had been waiting for the opportunity to join such an organization as the Ku Klux Klan.

In his sales pitch to Jim and Carole, Ken told them his most important project at the moment was "helping the poor, needy white families of Colorado Springs." He said he had received several calls from families needing assistance, but the citizens of Colorado Springs had not responded to his newspaper requests for financial assistance.

Ken said if necessary he would open up his own home to the needy white families for a Christmas dinner and he would also seek canned good donations from local supermarkets. He then launched into a speech about the current philosophy of the Ku Klux Klan. According to him, this "new" Klan was recharged in 1954 when they decided they no longer wanted their name connected with violence.

The "new" Klan, according to Ken, was now a political party and they hoped to soon run legal candidates in elections for the

U.S. Senate, the U.S. House of Representatives, and various state races for governor. It was, he said, David Duke's hope to run in the next general election for president of the United States. Ken's view that the "new Klan was now a political party" was in keeping with the strategy pursued by Duke regarding the changing of the Klan's traditionally held image as being just a bunch of ignorant, potbellied, beer-drinking, tobacco-chewing good ole southern boys.

Ken went on to say the Klan requested that all of its members become registered voters. He noted this was the way blacks gained political power over the years, by registering more voters to their cause and changing the political dynamic along the way. It was now time to put the Klan ideology into political action and reclaim the country.

Circling back to the topic of violence, Ken claimed he was not against violent and/or physical reprisals toward the Klan's enemies as long as the Klan name was not connected to such action.

At this point, Ken gave Jim and Carole applications to join the Ku Klux Klan, and this is where Jim almost took down the entire investigation. In his anxiety he signed his real name on the application, instead of Rick Kelley, his undercover alias. Carole was next to him, filling out her own application. Jim motioned to Chuck to come over, and he whispered to him, "I signed my real name. What do I do?"

"Crumple it up. Now. Then ask for another," Chuck said through clenched teeth.

So, Jim crumpled his application up and placed it in the garbage.

"Hey, Ken. Can I have another application? I messed mine up."

"Well, it can't be that bad. Let me see," said Ken.

"Ahh, I already threw it out. I'm sorry," said Jim. And Ken immediately went to the garbage and fished it out.

"No. No. No," said Jim, trying to be as nonchalant as he could while also desperately trying to make sure Ken didn't uncrumple the application and read his real name. "Can I just have a new one? I don't want to send in an application that's all wrinkled."

Ken paused, thought for a moment, then shrugged and said sure, but not before placing the crumpled application in his pocket.

Jim completed his and gave Ken the forty-five-dollar membership fee (from official CSPD funds) along with a Polaroid photo that had been taken in my office prior to leaving for the meeting.

Ken continued his personal testimony by acknowledging he was illegally carrying a handgun in his pocket and always carried one for protection. He said he did this because the Klan expected a race war to occur prior to the 1984 general elections, and he was preparing for it. He added that he had two shotguns, several rifles and pistols, with ammunition for all of them on hand for the race war. It was very clear that everyone in the Klan, and especially in the Posse, was crazy for guns.

The Colorado Springs Police Department's Intelligence Unit maintained a file on the Posse Comitatus and was well aware of their antigovernment, survivalist ideology. I, along with every member of our unit, knew their leader, Chuck Howarth. We spoke with him from time to time—rarely a cordial exchange—usually an anti–police authority confrontation that could easily escalate to deadly force.

When dealing with Howarth, we had to be on our guard

because he had a fascination with guns. He once questioned me during a contact I had with him about my personal .357 Magnum revolver, which I carried at the time, and how it compared to his preferred choice of a .45. Every time I tried to change the subject to the reason for my contacting him, he kept on his soliloquy until I finally, in as polite, respectful, and professional a tone as I could muster, told him to be quiet about guns and moved on to the purpose of my visit. On his property he often had a handgun on his hip, and on one occasion when I went to question him about a matter in which his name had come up, I and the officer with me had to order him to remove that gun before proceeding with our questioning. Was this constitutional? At that point we were not concerned about constitutional issues but rather about our (and his) safety; he had made numerous threats against CSPD officers; we were not going to take any chances with him. He removed the gun as "requested."

Ken then brought up the fact that he was leaving Colorado for approximately three years and Chuck had been voted to succeed him as the local organizer. Upon his return to Colorado Springs, he said, he intended to "raise hell."

At this point Ken began talking about his meeting with the Posse Comitatus. In an ironic twist he said he did not like the Posse because *they* were too radical and violent. If their members, however, still wanted to become Klansmen, he said he could not stop them, and, in fact, the Posse had services that could benefit the Klan. He pointed out that the two groups combined would total approximately fifty members.

Ken continued, explaining that the Posse wanted the military Klan members to steal automatic weapons and explosives from Fort Carson, and they would pay good money for them. Ken indicated he did not want his G.I. members engaged in this type of activity but expressed no outrage at the very thought of a direct sneak attack (i.e., theft) on a weapons/explosives cache from a U.S. military installation that flew the flag he had taken an oath to defend. He also said the Posse wanted to blow up some of the "queer" bars in town with hydrogen gas bombs filled with nails for a shrapnel-like maximum effect and seemed excited about the possibility.

The Posse's declaration of wanting to bomb "queer" bars— there were two gay bars/bathhouses in Colorado Springs at the time, the Hide N Seek Room Tavern (512 W. Colorado Avenue) and the Exit 21 Cocktail Lounge—did not strike Ken as alarming or in any way unusual, in spite of his personal affirmation as the local Klan leader that they were a nonviolent organization and did not condone such acts today as their forefathers had in the past. In one of my personal telephone conversations with Ken he had expressed the same notion as the Posse regarding the bombing of "queer" bars.

Posse members, according to Ken, were building cave houses for $20,000 in the mountains west of Colorado Springs in preparation for a nuclear attack. They were also storing food and weapons for such an eventuality. In summation, he felt the only good thing the Posse had to offer the Klan was their course on how to evade income taxes.

For Ken, the Posse was nothing more than a means to an end in terms of expanding the reach of the Klan because of their ideological similarities (i.e., a belief in white racial superiority, especially regarding Jews and blacks; a belief in ZOG—Zionist Occupied Government, that the Jews were behind a conspiracy to control the American government; a belief that government

taxation was unlawful to American citizens and they were obligated to and within their rights to evade paying any taxes; and
a belief that a racial war between whites and blacks was imminent and they should begin stockpiling weapons in preparation
for the coming conflict); as well as their knowledge of how to
exploit the government for tax purposes. Their marriage would
have been a match made in hell for the citizens of Colorado
Springs.

The meeting ended with Jim on the road to becoming a new
Klansman and providing me with a second undercover presence
of eyes and ears in the group as well as a backup support for
Chuck and vice versa. Ken invited them to attend a December 20
joint meeting between the Klan and the Posse at which time the
movie *The Birth of a Nation* would be shown.

On their way out, Jim asked Ken if he had a cigarette he could
bum. Ken felt around in his pockets, pulling out the crumpled
application along with a pack of smokes.

"Here, I'll take the smoke and that piece of garbage for you,"
said Jim. And with that he saved the investigation, and walked
into the night air breathing a sigh of relief.

7

KKKOLORADO

Now with Jim undercover the investigation was feeling like something much larger than my own pet project. The Posse Comitatus and the Klan were attempting to join forces, a marriage I certainly objected to. David Duke was to rally in the city in less than one month, and anti-Klan groups such as the Black Muslims, Black Panthers, and PLP were gathering a counterstorm that we were monitoring.

On December 16 the anti-Klan group People for the Betterment of People held a protest march in downtown Colorado Springs with approximately twenty participants. The People for the Betterment of People was, to be kind, not the best-organized group, but they were well intentioned. It was essentially organized by a concerned housewife in Colorado Springs who wanted to make a statement against hate in her community. They walked on the east side of Tejon Street from Vermijo Street. Marching counter to them on the west side of the street were Ken O'dell, wearing a Klan robe and carrying a Confederate flag, and his second in command, Joe Stewart, wearing a jacket with a KKK emblem.

At one point Ken gave brief interviews to the newspaper and television reporters, telling them they were not there to create confrontation. He even explained the presence of only two Klansmen as an effort to stress the nonviolent aspect of the organization as well as to keep the identities of Klan members secret.

I personally monitored the march by walking alongside Ken and Joe close enough to hear any personal conversation they might exchange between them. Several times, I laughed to myself that the "Ron Stallworth" Ken often talked to on the phone was standing within three feet of him and he never realized the truth of the hoax being played out against him and his cohorts. I was always cautious about the people around me, whether someone would recognize me and call out "Detective Stallworth" or "Ron Stallworth," which would alert Ken and start him questioning why this black cop's name was the same as that of the Klansman he had personally selected to replace him as local organizer. I did not say anything and made myself as inconspicuous as possible throughout the march. I was actually enjoying the paradox that I, a "loyal and dedicated Klansman," was standing three feet from the man who recommended me as his replacement.

One interesting exchange that struck home occurred during the march. We were witnesses to a new day and attitudes toward the Ku Klux Klan. While stopped at an intersection red light, a black man holding his five-year-old son's hand stopped beside me and was standing next to O'dell. The son looked at Ken curiously, pointed to him, and asked his father, "Daddy, why is that man dressed so funny?"

I started chuckling along with the others standing nearby

when the father, looking directly at Ken, replied, "He's just a damn clown, son."

Ken and Joe glared at the father and those of us laughing as the light turned green and the march continued for a couple more blocks to its conclusion.

The response of the father convinced me we were in the dawn of a new era. For a black man in years past to openly refer to a robed Klansman as a "clown" would have been a futile and foolhardy statement of defiance, ignorance, or stupidity. Here in 1978 Colorado Springs, the father showed bold courage by openly challenging the white-robed, Confederate flag symbolism and, while looking Ken straight in the eye, declared to his son and all those around, he was nothing more than a "clown." A few decades earlier and the result would probably have been a death sentence for the father.

As I said, the rally wasn't the best organized. It lasted about forty-five minutes, ending with a few speeches and a small crowd milling about trying to hear.

While we prepared for Duke's arrival several interesting events happened within the investigation to further it along. First, I received a phone call from Ken inviting me to participate in a Klan cross burning ceremony. He said he was still working out the details in terms of a date, time, and location but he wanted me to be aware of the plan and ready to participate at the appropriate time. I told him I eagerly awaited further news of the cross burning, in particular the location. I asked if he had a specific place in mind to plant the cross. He replied that planning had not progressed that far yet, but he assured me it would be at a strategic location in Colorado Springs where everyone, for miles around and in every direction, would be able to see the flames and know that the Klan presence was alive and well in the city. He wanted me to be involved in the cross burning ceremony because it was a "deeply moving religious experience."

Second, I had established contact with the RAC (Resident Agent-in-Charge), of the Colorado Springs FBI Office regarding any intelligence assistance the Bureau could provide for me on the Ku Klux Klan. I was seeking general background information, in particular historical data of the group in Colorado. As a police officer I knew that the FBI maintained a treasure trove of information on organizations and individuals, though they did not like to acknowledge that fact, and I wanted what they had on the history of Colorado's Klan past.

The RAC, a good friend who became a valuable ally in my investigation, had a colorful past as a federal government agent and, if his stories were to be believed, had a history of his own with the Klan. He had a gift for gab and his tales were full of hyperbole so it was hard to separate the wheat from the chaff, not to mention he always punctuated them with the fact that the full nature of the information was still highly "classified" by the government. He had worked for the CIA for a while before switching to the FBI back in the J. Edgar Hoover era, and he often regaled us with his James Bondian tales of clandestine work for "The Company" (CIA) and FBI. We would only be given cursory information, enough to whet our appetites; then he would give us the gist of the story and more often than not a bellyaching laugh for all of us at his recollection of events, without revealing what he claimed was still "classified information."

One of his tales concerned the 1964 murder case of three civil rights workers in Mississippi. The three were reported missing and the FBI was sent to rural Neshoba County to investigate, only to find that the sheriff's office was linked to the local Ku Klux Klan. The agents were unable to talk to the white people in the community because of their sympathy for and fear of the Klan and hatred for federal government authority. They were also unable to talk to the members of the black community because of their natural fear of the Klan born out of generations of inbred terror.

The lead agent, a northerner, believed in following FBI investigative protocol and ran into a brick wall of silence. His assistant, a southerner who knew the nature of the people because he had at one time been like them and understood southern culture, advocated an alternative "outside-the-box" approach to the investigation that violated protocol. They eventually followed that approach and developed an informant who broke the case wide open, leading them to the bodies of the murder victims. The FBI ended up arresting several KKK members, including the sheriff. The case was immortalized in the movie *Mississippi Burning* starring Academy Award–winning actor Gene Hackman as the southern FBI agent.

The Colorado Springs RAC told me he was part of the FBI team that worked that case, and they were under direct orders from J. Edgar Hoover to solve it. It wasn't until they deviated from constitutional protocol, some of which is depicted in the movie or in scenes that were composites of events that actually happened, that they were able to secure the evidence culminating in the arrests of the murderers of the slain civil rights workers.

I asked the RAC to help me through his government connections to obtain the history of the Klan in Colorado. He jokingly replied that the FBI regional headquarters in Denver did not have any information on the KKK.

I fired back that the FBI kept files on everybody and everything. He shook his head, laughed, and walked away.

He came to the Detective Division several times a week, and whenever our paths crossed I posed the same request: "Get me the FBI files on the history of the Colorado Klan." Each time he would shake his head at me, smile, and walk away, though I noticed that the outright denial of the existence of the information had stopped.

After a couple of weeks of this type of exchange—this game— the RAC approached me one day in my office and put a piece of paper in my hand that had the name and phone number of an FBI agent assigned to the Denver office. The RAC told me Agent X was expecting my call.

I asked who Agent X was and why he was expecting my call. The RAC's response was a simple smile and the words, "Make the call, you bastard." No further discourse or explanation, just a deep air of mystery. This, however, was not unusual for the RAC, who, based on his professional history, often spoke in cryptic terms, leaving the listener to ponder the underlying motivation and meaning of his statement and whether or not it was based on hyperbole or fact.

The next day I phoned Agent X, who said he had heard about my "rather unique" investigation. He laughed at the hilarity of the hoax that I had been perpetrating on the Klan members and their mindless stupidity at falling for the antics we had unleashed. He congratulated me on the valuable intelligence information that was pouring in as a result of the investigation. But before I could explain what I needed, he told me to come to his Denver office the next day. No further details were offered on his part, and our conversation ended.

The next afternoon I finally met Agent X. He escorted me to a conference room and told me to have a seat at the large rectangular brown wooden conference table. He left me alone for about three minutes and when he returned he was carrying a couple of pencils and a legal pad in his left hand. In his right hand was an expandable folder approximately six inches wide, filled with papers. These items were placed on the table in front of me with instructions that I could look at anything in the folder and write down notes, but absolutely no copies of any of the material were allowed out of the room. He told me to take my time and then left me alone.

Inside the folder was a treasure trove of data on the history of the Ku Klux Klan in Colorado. Many of the sheets of paper were yellowed with age and dated back to the 1920s. It was a virtual time capsule on the Colorado Klan: how and when they formed (1921); their first Grand Dragon, a physician named John Galen Locke; and their activities, such as bombing the home of a black mail carrier who had moved into a white neighborhood, burning a black A.M.E.—African Methodist Episcopal—church to the ground, boycotting Denver's Jewish businessmen and excluding them from being members of specific clubs such as the Masons, and making physical threats to Jews and Catholics.

By 1923 it was estimated that the Klan in Colorado had approximately thirty thousand to forty-five thousand members, half of whom lived in Denver. There were also chapters in Canon City, home of the state penitentiary; Boulder, home of the University of Colorado; Colorado Springs; and Pueblo, about thirty-five miles south of Colorado Springs. Once established, the Klan made a grasp for political power. They took control of the state's Republican Party and selected virtually all of its candidates in the 1924 elections. By 1925, the Colorado State Senate and House of Representatives were filled with a majority of Klan members elected through the Republican Party.

What immediately leaped out of the yellowed pages at me was the name Benjamin Stapleton, one of their candidates. He was elected mayor of Denver and served from 1923 to 1947. He was the major force behind a project which later became the Denver Municipal Airport. In 1944 the airport's name was changed in his honor to Stapleton International Airport.

Several key members of his mayoral staff were also Klan members. So committed was his relationship to the Klan that irate voters called for his resignation after learning of his Klan sympathies, which he withheld during the campaign. His response to their recall effort was delivered at a Klan rally:

"I pledge to work with the Klan and for the Klan in the coming election, heart and soul, and if I am elected I shall give the Klan the kind of administration it wants."

Stapleton won the recall election on the strength of the large Klan voter turnout and their influence on the Denver populace. Jubilant in their victory, Klan members held a cross burning ceremony.

In the November 1924 general election other Klan-supported candidates swept to victory. The governor, Clarence J. Morley, was a Klansman; the two U.S. senators, Rice Means and Lawrence Phipps, had strong Klan connections; and the Klan held the offices of lieutenant governor, state auditor, and attorney general. Another Klansman, William J. Candlish, was selected by the Grand Dragon to be the chief of police for the Denver Police

Department and was officially appointed by Mayor Stapleton. In addition, Klansmen were seated on the Board of Regents for the University of Colorado and the State Supreme Court. The City of Denver and State of Colorado, in essence, were under Klan control. So pervasive was the Klan's control and influence in Colorado that certain national publications began spelling Colorado with a *K*. Their political dominance lasted approximately three years, ending in 1926 following funding irregularities investigated by federal authorities.

I sat at the conference table for close to two hours, fascinated by what I was reading, taking as many notes as I could, shocked and fascinated with the vast richness of the information. I was literally reading about and seeing images of ghosts who had changed Colorado society, some for the better because of their politics, others in a negative way because of their social leanings. A thought kept going through my mind: *I wonder how many people who fly in and out of Stapleton International Airport know that, in their own way, they are paying homage to a past leader of the Ku Klux Klan.* I had frequented the airport many times and up until that very moment had no hint of its historical connection to the Klan.

Much of the Klan's approach from half a century earlier was being, or trying to be, revived by today's generation of Klansmen. Their takeover of an entire capital city, Denver, and the state government was the precedent that motivated Ken O'dell's talk of the Klan becoming a political party and of registering Klan members to vote.

I recorded several pages of notes from the file, which Agent X reminded me with a smile that I had not seen. He cautioned me that my use of any of the information I had just discovered could not refer back to the FBI because the file did not officially exist. I acknowledged his concerns and then returned to my office in Colorado Springs.

A day or two after my return from Denver, I received a package at my office from a congressional investigator with the U.S. House of Representatives. Inside the package were four volumes of "Hearings on Activities of Ku Klux Klan Organizations in the United States of the House of Representatives Committee on Un-American Activities of the 89th Congress (1965–66)." It contained an entire "official" history of the Klan based on a federal government inquiry during the height of the civil rights movement, including witness testimony and official Klan documentation. It provided good background information on the Klan to help me further understand the organization and the type of people attracted to its ideological brand.

I do not know how these volumes were sent to my attention.

I established contact with the executive director of the Denver-based Jewish group Anti-Defamation League of B'nai B'rith (ADL). The ADL is an organization dedicated to monitoring and combating white supremacists or any other group that supports a belief in racial superiority and dominance, in particular those that are anti-Semitic. When I told Barbara Coppersmith of the ADL about my investigation and the information support I was seeking, she was at first amused by it all and then pledged to assist me in any way possible with any ADL resources out of the Denver office and, if necessary, from their national offices in New York City. I, in turn, agreed to keep her informed on a regular basis as to any new developments in the investigation. From that point on I began receiving ADL material on the Klan, all of historical value, and some intelligence because of their network of sources.

This was another example of "outside-the-box" thinking. In general civilians, unless they are directly involved in an investigation and have a need to know specific details, are kept out of the loop of the official actions being taken by police investigators. In this case I made the decision, based on past history of the Klan's attitude and relationship with America's Jewish community, that Coppersmith and the ADL could be a valuable ally. I therefore kept her regularly informed of events, occasionally withholding certain details, and she, in turn, kept forwarding me ADL literature on the Klan, both in Colorado and a cross the country, so that I remained abreast of any new trends.

On the matter of "new trends," Coppersmith would ask me from time to time if I could ask my Klan "sources" about this or that issue, things that the ADL in Denver had developed information on or been asked by other ADL offices around the country to check into. I would then place a telephone call to either Ken O'dell or Fred Wilkens or both and steer the conversation to that particular issue. I would relay their response and on a couple of occasions phoned David Duke and spoke with him, and he unwittingly cooperated with his archenemy— an organization he more than once told me he despised—by giving me an answer to their question. Barbara Coppersmith was an elderly lady and would often exclaim, "My, oh my, what fun," and there were moments when it was. She derived great pleasure in knowing that the Grand Wizard of the KKK was "cooperating" with an ADL inquiry/investigation. She loved the intrigue of being a part of our "sting" against the Klan and enjoyed receiving periodic updates on newly obtained information.

My friendship, for lack of a better word, with David Duke was only strengthening. Following my December 12 conversation with him, we began speaking roughly one to two times a week. I would call him to praise him. I'd always call him "Mr. Duke" and say it looked like the Klan was really doing great. And then he'd go on and explain all their plans, bragging and boasting and feeding me information.

For example, in separate conversations Duke told me of planned Klan marches in Los Angeles, Kansas City, and other areas of the country. In the conversations he would provide details as to their rally point, specific objectives of their rally, planned counterresponse measures, which were always violence-based in spite of their claim to being a nonviolent group, and efforts against police response. As soon as possible after such conversations I would call the appropriate law enforcement agency in that city's jurisdictional area and alert them to Duke's information. Several times in follow-up conversations Duke would convey his surprise at how well prepared certain police agencies were to the Klan's presence, almost as if they knew beforehand what was going to happen.

I would call Duke at the request of other agencies from around the country, including the FBI, whose policy as a result of fallout from post-Watergate reforms, forbid them from addressing the activities of the Klan or any group unless events indicated a violent or conspiratorial threat; agency representatives investigating subversive groups from an intelligence perspective learning of the undercover investigation into Duke's organization would break out in side-splitting laughter after finding out specifics of the investigation—a black cop pulling off an undercover "sting" of the Ku Klux Klan.

A couple requests came from the New Orleans Police Department, which had been unable to successfully penetrate Duke's organization with an undercover officer or an informant. These opportunities opened the door for me to expand my line of questioning in different directions. Sometimes my conversations with David Duke were light, personal discussions about his wife, Chloe, and their children. How they were doing and what was going on in their lives. He always responded with cordial enthusiasm like the proud and loving husband and father he was. He was more than willing to share tales of the beauty of their being. As a matter of fact, when you took away the topic of white supremacy and KKK nonsense from discourse with Duke, he was a very pleasant conversationalist. He seemed like a "regular" guy. Once that topic entered the margins of Klan ideology, however, Dr. Jekyll became Mr. Hyde and the monster in him was unleashed. He once told me that his wife was a partner in his Klan experience and his children were being raised in the Klan world under the tutelage of the Klan Youth Corps.

At times, my conversation was educational with a racist comical tone to it. I once asked "Mr. Duke," everyone referred to him respectfully as "Mister," if he was ever concerned about some smart-aleck "nigger" calling him while pretending to be white. He replied, "No, I can always tell when I'm talking to a nigger." When I asked him how he could tell, he said the following: "Take you, for example. I can tell that you're a pure

Aryan white man by the way you talk, the way you pronounce certain words and letters."

I asked him to be more specific and he said, "A white man pronounces the English language the way it was meant to be pronounced. For example take the word 'are' or the letter 'r.' A pure Aryan like you or I say it the proper way, 'are,' whereas a nigger would pronounce it 'are-uh.' Niggers do not have the same intelligence as the white man to properly speak English the way it was meant to be spoken. Whenever you talk to someone on the phone and are unfamiliar with them, always listen to their speech pattern for a short while to determine how they pronounce certain words." He never told me what those other words were.

I replied in as flattering a tone as I could muster, without laughing or getting sick, "Mr. Duke, I want to thank you for this lesson because if you had not brought it to my attention I would never have noticed the difference between how we talk and how niggers talk. From now on I'm going to pay close attention to my telephone conversations to make sure I'm not talking to one of 'them' [a nigger]."

He seemed humbled and pleased by my fawning over his gracious nature in sharing his knowledge and "wisdom." He told me he was glad to help and hoped this lesson was beneficial. From that point on, whenever I spoke to Duke on the phone I always found a point in the conversation to inject a question that incorporated the word "are" in it except I would pronounce it like a "nigger," "are-uh." This was my symbolic way of sticking a finger in Duke's eye and an extended middle finger in his face to show him that this high school–educated black man with only twenty college credits was smarter than he, a college graduate with a master's degree. My use of the "are-uh" was my way of playing with his head and having a little fun at his expense. He never picked up on the fact that one of his pure Aryan white Klansmen was speaking English like a "nigger" and was, in fact, a proud black man of African descent.

Duke's assessment of blacks' use of language was interesting in that he was only partially right. Some blacks from the South do, in fact, pronounce the word "are" in the manner in which he described. An example was my late mother-in-law. She was born and bred in Alabama, a graduate of Alabama State University with a master's degree in business, and was a retired head of the Business Department at a Colorado Springs high school. She was active in her A.M.E. (African Methodist Episcopal) church and black community affairs, yet throughout my thirty-year experience with her she pronounced the word "are" exactly as described by David Duke.

The racial fallacy in his argument is that this pronunciation is not unique to blacks. Many people from the South, whites included, employ this speech pattern. In other words, it has nothing to do with pure Aryan white racial intelligence superiority as stated by the Grand Wizard, but rather is more of a regional reflection of a cultural linguistic upbringing. In other words, his logic was extremely flawed and unsubstantiated by facts.

Another significant factor about this particular conversation was Duke's freewheeling use of the pejorative "nigger." He was publicizing himself at the time and being reported by the media as being the "new face of the modern Klan." He was not the stereotypical, uneducated, potbellied, tobacco-chewing/spitting, beer-guzzling Klansman of movie lore. David Duke was respectable-looking, always appearing in public in a suit and tie; he wore his Klan robe only for private ceremonial purposes. He was educated, holding a master's degree in political science from Louisiana State University, well spoken, and an excellent debater. He was the "new" Klan leader. His image and public persona reflected that of his Klan organization. He and they did not use "nigger" in public but freely threw it out among themselves in private.

In one of my conversations with Duke, we talked politics and he told me of his intention to run for elective office in the near future. He explained that only by changing the political landscape through the ballot box could the Klan hope to change conditions in America to be more beneficial to the white race. He would run for a Louisiana state office first but eventually would take a shot at the presidency.

It is interesting to take a closer look at Duke's political leanings in 1978 and 1979. Though he listed himself as a conservative Democrat at the time, he did not change his party affiliation to Republican for nearly ten years. Much of his political thinking, as in his world in general, revolved around the issue of race. In that world whites were more intelligent than and overall superior to blacks and other minority groups. He believed that the white race was the defender of America's virtue and its values and the Klan was the physical embodiment of that defense. His views were more suited for an America that existed during the years of the Eisenhower presidency (1953 to 1961), a period when white dominance in America was the norm and the Klan literally ruled communities across the South.

That era, which included Wisconsin senator Joe McCarthy and his crusade against communism, was one of an attitude of "cultural elitism" on the part of the white mainstream. That attitude was very notable in the attack back then against rock 'n' roll, the new form of music that was emerging from the roots of black culture and being widely accepted by white youth. The Klan played key roles in denouncing this emerging trend and tried to suppress its continued influence among white youth.

That thinking from over a half century ago, that political perspective and the words used to describe an emerging cultural trend that ran contrary to the white mainstream of the time, found a rebirth in the actions and words of the modern conservative movement.

When I see the news today, news that reminds me a great deal of my time investigating the Klan, I like to think of that father and son, walking next to Ken in his Klan outfit. It's just some clown.

Stallworth at the age of twenty-two (1975). The first black detective
in the history of the Colorado Springs Police Department.

Stallworth's Colorado Springs Police ID—with proper
fitting cap.

TOWARDS A PROGRESSIVE
AFRICAN
WORLD

STOKELY CARMICHAEL
SPEAKS!

Wednesday, April 20, ████—7:00 P.M.
Bell's Nightingale   601 E. Las Vegas

AFRICAN STYLE SHOW
MUSIC/DANCING
HORS D'OEUVRES

TOWARDS A PROGRESSIVE AFRICAN WORLD!

A-APRP

Donation:
$3.00

Sponsored By:
A-APRP

Ticket to "Stokely Carmichael Speaks" event.

Gazette-Telegraph coverage of Stokely's speech.

Knights of the Ku Klux Klan

MEMBERSHIP APPLICATION

I believe in the ideals of Western, Christian Civilization and Culture, in the White race that created them and in the Constitution of the United States.

I am a White person of non-Jewish descent, 18 years of age or older.

I believe in the aims and objectives of the Knights of the Ku Klux Klan.

I swear that I will keep secret and confidential any information I receive in quest of membership.

I certify that I meet all requirements above under the penalty of perjury if falsified.

INITIATION FEE   A one-time initiation fee of $15 is required when applying for membership in the Knights of the Ku Klux Klan. When a man and wife both join at the same time, there is only one $15 fee required for both. Students are not required to pay this $15 initiation fee.

Attached is my Initiation (naturalization) fee ($15. minimum) _____.

KLAN DUES.   Klan members are required to pay an annual membership fee of $30. This covers both a man and his wife. Annual dues for students is $15. When your annual fee is paid in full you will receive your passport and an attractive certificate for the current year. You will also receive a detailed Klan handbook outlining Klan history and Klan conduct.

Your annual membership fee also entitles you to receive the official publication of the Knights of the Ku Klux Klan, the *Crusader*, as well as the official internal bulletin, *KKK Action*.

If you join in Jan/Feb/Mar/April, your membership dues are	$30 _____
If you join in May/June/July/Aug, your membership dues for the remainder of the year are	$20 _____
If you join in Sep/Oct/Nov/Dec, your membership dues for the remainder of the year are	$10 ✓

Each month I will try to contribute: ☐ $5   ☒ $10   ☐ $25   ☐ $50   ☐ $100   ☐ $ _____

When you apply for membership in the Knights of the Ku Klux Klan, your initiation fee of $15 must be paid. You cannot be naturalized into the Klan until this has been paid. Those persons applying for membership who are not required to pay this initiation fee must pay their dues with this application.

Name (Please print clearly) RON STALLWORTH

Address P.O. BOX 4945

City COLO. SPGS.   State COLO. Zip 80930 Phone (303) 633-4498

Birth date 6-18-53   Occupation PUBLIC UTILITIES

Any talents which might be useful to this movement?   Explain _____

I certify that the photograph and information presented herein is genuine and accurate. I understand that any misrepresentations on this application for membership will result in this application being declared null and void.

Make all checks payable to:
Patriot Press   Box 624   Metairie, LA 70004

Signature of Applicant

Ron Stallworth
11-13-78   Date

LOCAL UNIT ADDRESS:
Ken
PO Box 4771
Colo Springs Co 80930

"Ron Stallworth's" application to join the KKK.

1865   1979

RON STALLWORTH   CO 78862

Member in Good Standing for the Year 1979.

Knights of the Ku Klux Klan

Membership card to the Ku Klux Klan.

2 Springs Marches Peaceful

By PATRICK O'GRADY
GT Staff Writer

People for the Betterment of People, an organization opposed to the formation of a local Ku Klux Klan chapter, conducted a peaceful, announced, northerly march up the east sidewalk of Tejon Street Saturday.

So did the Klan, but in a much smaller, unannounced version.

As Peggy Rizo's fledgling 20-plus member organization walked slowly along the east sidewalk, Josef Stewart and Kenneth O'Dell, members of the Colorado Springs chapter of the KKK, walked along the west sidewalk.

O'Dell, the highest-ranking local Klansman, was bedecked in full robes and carrying a Confederate flag. Stewart wore civilian clothes. Both men are soldiers stationed at Fort Carson, and the only publicly-revealed Klansmen here aside from press secretary Butch Blakeman.

Prior to the anti-Klan march — which attracted some two dozen people, black, white and brown — Ms. Rizo outlined her reasons for the demonstration.

"I just really got tired of it," she said, speaking of local media coverage of the newly-formed Klan den. "This is my home; if they can voice that they want members, then I can voice my opinions, too, that I don't want them here.

"I think the KKK and people like them are a backward step for mankind," Ms. Rizo continued. "We're just trying to institute higher thoughts."

Both PBP and KKK spokespersons have said several times in the past that they are nonviolent and merely wish to make their opinions known, rather than create confrontations. O'Dell and Stewart said they showed up Saturday to prove their nonviolent credo.

"We're just here to show we're nonviolent," O'Dell said, marching with the Stars and Bars held prominently before him.

O'Dell said the reason only two Klansmen appeared was to stress the nonviolent aspect of the organization as well as keep the identities of Klan members secret.

Across the street, anti-Klan marchers told why they turned out in the windy 15-degree weather. "They used to burn crosses on our property," said a tearful Helen Riordan, speaking of her days in a small community in upstate New York where she said the KKK made Irish-Catholics part of their target.

"I think it's sad — people on that level where they are really divided," said Jennifer Parisi. She also said she felt the march was not done in negative fashion, against the KKK, but rather in the spirit of trying to promote more positive relations between people.

Ms. Parisi added that the organization hopes to conduct "some kind of rally or symposium" to coincide with Martin Luther King Day.

● Marches Peaceful

From Page 1A

is right for you and you hope that it makes things better."

The local Klan had talked of trying to organize a December march but never applied for a permit. Ms. Rizo's group needed no permit because it was a sidewalk march, single-file, rather than a parade down the street. Local KKK plans now are for its own march after the first of the year, timed to coincide with Grand Wizard David Duke's tour of the Pikes Peak Region.

"Mr. Duke is the brains of our organization," Stewart said, adding that Duke, based at KKK headquarters in New Orleans, already is scheduled for several appearances on local television.

GT Photo by Dale Allen
Bullhorn in hand, Peggy Rizo led anti-Klan march
Supporters went single-file on Tejon Street with signs

Ken in full hood and robe at an anti-Klan protest.

Card that the Fort Carson soldier threw on the ground at the Bunny Club when he threatened to "firebomb this place."

Progressive Labor Party flyer.

Knights Of The
Ku Klux Klan

CERTIFICATE OF CITIZENSHIP
AWARDED TO

RON STALLWORTH

BE IT KNOWN TO ALL MEN OF HONOR, TO LOVERS OF LAW AND ORDER, PEACE AND JUSTICE, RACIAL INTEGRITY AND WHITE CULTURE, THAT THIS INDIVIDUAL HAS STEPPED FORWARD AND DISTINGUISHED HIMSELF THROUGH HIS QUEST FOR CITIZENSHIP IN THE INVISIBLE EMPIRE, AND BY HIS UNSWERVING DUTY TO THE BETTERMENT OF OUR PEOPLE AND NATION. UPON THIS DAY THIS PERSON OF HONOR HAS BEEN DULY APPOINTED TO THE RANK OF. . .

KLANSMAN

LET ALL KLANSMEN OF THE INVISIBLE EMPIRE, KNIGHTS OF THE KU KLUX KLAN TAKE DUE NOTICE OF THIS CITIZENSHIP AND GOVERN THEMSELVES ACCORDINGLY. THIS AWARDED CITIZENSHIP HOLDS FOR A PERIOD OF THE CALENDAR YEAR IN WHICH IT IS ISSUED OR UNTIL REVOKED BY THE ISSUING OFFICER OR EQUIVALENT AUTHORITY.

JANUARY 19, 1979
DATE ISSUED

WITNESSED

DAVID DUKE
GRAND WIZARD

Stallworth's certificate of citizenship to the KKK.

— PERSONAL CODE —
KNIGHTS OF THE KU KLUX KLAN

I PLEDGE

1. to untiringly work for the preservation, protection, and advancement of the White race
2. to forever be loyal to the Knights of the Ku Klux Klan — as the only true Klan
3. to obey all orders from officers of the Empire
4. to keep secret all fellow members and Klan rituals
5. to never discuss any Klan affairs with any plain clothes officers on a state, local or national level
6. fulfill social, fraternal, and financial obligations to this order as long as I live

Signature

National Director   Date

The KKK personal code.

(*above*) Chuck with David Duke. (*below*) David Duke with Jim (far right), Chuck (second from right), and other inductees.

The entrance to NORAD.

Civil rights activist Ralph Abernathy pictured here at a rally in the rain at Dexter Avenue Baptist Church to commemorate Martin Luther King Jr. one year after his assassination.

8

INDUCTION

On December 20 Jim received a phone call from Ken to check for assurance that he and Chuck would be at his house at seven o'clock that evening for a showing of *The Birth of a Nation*. In addition, he wanted their help moving lumber that was intended for the construction of crosses for burning ceremonies. He explained that one of the crosses was going to be thirty feet high and burned in Denver soon.

Ken said that within a week the Colorado Springs chapter was going to burn a cross on a hill near the intersection of Hancock and Delta, a strategic, highly populated thoroughfare. He also revealed that Fred Wilkens would be attending the meeting. Ken informed Jim that he and Chuck would be personally nationalized, meaning sworn in as official members of the Ku Klux Klan by David Duke in January during his visit to the Colorado Springs area.

So when I found out the exact information of when and where Ken and the Klan were planning on burning a cross, I would do several things. I would notify the commander in charge and request that dispatchers send extra units to constantly patrol the area of the intersection where the burning was to take place, in this instance of Hancock and Delta. We'd have two or three cars cruising in that area, looking out for anyone who would be planting a cross.

We wouldn't know that the Klan was actually doing something, because it would be a crime we prevented through our presence rather than planting a trap to sting them, and catch them red-handed.

Ken continued, stating he had met an elderly man who had been an active member of the Klan in the 1920s and 1930s. He confirmed this man's Klan past because he knew the "secret handshake" of the Klan. It was this man's intention to reactivate his membership and help the Colorado Springs chapter grow. Ken closed by stating that Jim and Chuck would be taught the secret Klan handshake after they had been nationalized by David Duke.

The phone call ended, and we all started laughing. First they got their ideas about how to light a cross from a James Bond movie, and now they were bragging about secret handshakes. It was as if Dennis the Menace were running a hate group.

At 7:00 P.M., Chuck and Jim attended the joint meeting between the Klan and the Posse Comitatus held at a Westside Colorado Springs residence. The purpose of the meeting was for leaders of the two groups to exchange ideas on maximizing collaboration.

Along with Chuck and Jim in their undercover roles, representing the Klan were Fred Wilkens and David Lane, the Denver organizer and an attorney who said he represented the Klan in the greater Denver area. This was the first time we had encountered David Lane other than seeing his name referenced in an occasional media story on the hate movement in Colorado. Also representing the Klan was Donald Black, the Alabama state organizer/Grand Dragon, who was a close associate of Duke's and had been visiting Wilkens, his counterpart, in Colorado. He agreed to accompany him to this meeting, though we did not know if it was to support Wilkens or if he was in Colorado on behalf of the national office of the Knights of the Ku Klux Klan on orders from Duke. Also from Denver was an individual representing the American Nazi Party.

Donald Black is an interesting figure in the history of the racist/hate movement. When Duke left the Klan around 1980 to form the National Association for the Advancement of White People (NAAWP), Black took over as Grand Wizard of the Knights of the Ku Klux Klan. He was unsuccessful in sustaining the "respectable" image initiated by Duke. According to the Southern Poverty Law Center's Klanwatch Project, about a year after Black assumed control of the Knights of the Ku Klux Klan he was arrested along with other Klansmen and neo-Nazis for attempting to overthrow the government of Dominica. Years later, after Duke and his wife divorced, Black married Duke's ex-wife and they founded the internet's first hate site, Stormfront.org.

This meeting was the first time we learned of a link between the Klan and the American Nazi Party in Colorado Springs. Also in attendance were the Colorado Springs Klan members Tim and Joe, and new prospective members, including the elderly man who had supposedly been a Klansman in the 1920s to 1930s. Representing the Posse were its leader, Chuck Howarth, and several other members. The attorney took control of the meeting by urging the Posse to become more actively involved in white racist groups in Colorado.

Ken told Wilkens he had recruited thirty-eight prospective Klan members in the Colorado State Penitentiary. He asked Wilkens if he had accomplished anything regarding the circulation of the Klan newspaper at Fort Carson. Wilkens replied that the military authorities had not yet contacted him regarding the request to circulate *The Crusader* on base.

Donald Black then introduced the film *The Birth of a Nation* to the audience. At intermission, the Denver contingent announced they were going to leave; however, before they did, the attorney gave his "closing argument" for uniting the two groups by stating, "All white groups must unite in order to be successful in their efforts to obtain white supremacy." He urged everyone present to join the local Ku Klux Klan. He ended his statement with the Nazi greeting, the raised right arm with hand open, palm down, and a hearty "Sieg Heil."

My contact at the Anti-Defamation League, Barbara Coppersmith, was very interested in this meeting when I relayed the events to her and the attorney's particular role in it. She indicated to me that she would be notifying her headquarters office in New York City with the information because they would be very concerned by this attempt to merge the Klan with the Posse Comitatus. She further indicated that my investigation had uncovered something that they had not previously been aware of.

After the Denver men's departure, the second half of the film was viewed by the Colorado Springs residents. After the showing, Posse leader Chuck Howarth ordered twenty-four copies of the Klan newspapers for his members. The meeting ended shortly thereafter. It was Jim's opinion that the Klan and Posse leaders had been receptive to their respective philosophies and a follow-up meeting was set for a future date in Denver.

Back at the station we later discussed what had happened that evening. To Chuck and Jim, it was clear that the two groups were getting along just fine, like peanut butter and jelly, and that the threat of their merger was more relevant and real than ever before.

On January 2, 1979, my Ku Klux Klan membership card was delivered by the U.S. Postal Service to Ken's residence. Jim met with him to pick it up and it was later given to me.

As promised, the card had the two letters "CO" on it to denote that my membership was in Colorado. It was followed by a number starting with 78, for 1978, the year of my joining, and 862, meaning I was the 862nd registered Klansman in Colorado.

While at Ken's home, Jim was told that he and Chuck should arrive at his house at 1:30 P.M. on January 7 to be "nationalized," officially inducted into the Knights of the Ku Klux Klan by David Duke, who would arrive in Denver the day before. He explained that fifteen members from Colorado Springs would be going through the "nationalization" ceremony. He also indicated that Fred Wilkens was scheduled to be at his home later this evening to discuss the details of Duke's visit. Ken further stated that he and a local television station had gained permission from Fort Carson authorities to interview white people on the base regarding prejudice against white soldiers.

The meeting ended with Jim returning to the police department with my membership card, which I immediately signed. The part of the card that grabbed my attention was the back side, with its "six pledges" concerning the "Personal Code" of the Knights of the Ku Klux Klan.

PERSONAL CODE

1. To untiringly work for the preservation, protection, and advancement of the white race
2. To forever be loyal to the Knights of the Ku Klux Klan—as the only true Klan
3. To obey all orders from the officers of the Empire
4. To keep secret all fellow members and Klan rituals
5. To never discuss any Klan affairs with any plain clothes officers on a state, local or national level
6. Fulfill social, fraternal, and financial obligations to this order as long as I live

The pledge that captured my attention and drove me, Jim, and Chuck into a fit of laughter was number 5: *"I Pledge: to never discuss any Klan affairs with any plain clothes officers on a state, local or national level."* That was almost too good— they actually put that right there on their membership card.

After receiving the card, I placed two calls: the first to Ken and the second to David Duke. I thanked Ken for having my membership card delivered to me. He was gracious in his response but explained that though my membership had been registered with the national office in Louisiana, it would not be finalized until I had gone through the nationalization ceremony.

"It's a technicality, but it's important. I think you'll like the ceremony," he said.

Ken went on to explain that a Denver-area location had been

reserved for the ceremony and following that, *The Birth of a Nation* would be shown yet again. He said the location had a seating capacity of 150 and 113 invitations had already been sent to Denver-area residents to come witness the ceremony and to celebrate Duke's visit, adding they expected to fill all 150 seats because, in addition to the ceremony and film, Duke would be giving a speech.

He continued that once Duke's Colorado Springs visit was concluded he wanted the local membership to hold a cross-burning ceremony. He explained how on either the eleventh or twelfth of January a hole would be dug in the ground and a cross doused with kerosene would be placed in it somewhere in the Sand Creek area (east) near Academy Boulevard, which is close to Interstate 25 and thus highly visible to passing motorists.

Igniting the cross, he said, would be accomplished by using a "matchbook" fuse, a method he once saw done in a Bond movie: it entailed placing a book of matches at the base of the cross and sticking a lit cigarette—burned down until it had about two minutes left—in the matchbook. When the lit end made contact with the matches they would ignite and, in turn, ignite the cross. By lighting the cross in this way, Ken explained, it would give them time to put some distance between them and the burning cross before the police arrived on the scene in response to citizen complaints. I made note of the location, where I would be sending patrol units.

I asked Ken if wearing a hooded robe was required for those being nationalized. He replied that it was not mandatory; however, if I had one I should wear it, as it helped promote a sense of Klan pride. We did not purchase a Klan robe from the national office because the police department would not authorize the forty-dollar expense. After Ken told me Duke would be in Colorado Springs on January 10, our conversation ended.

I was never able to secure the forty dollars, eighty if we include the cost of Jim's robe, from Sergeant Trapp. The fee was just too high and my pleas that it would legitimize both Chuck and Jim were not convincing enough.

I then placed a phone call to Duke down in Louisiana. I thanked him profusely for approving my membership into "his" Klan and told him how proud I was to finally have my membership card. He cordially accepted my words of gratitude and said he looked forward to my continued participation as a Klansman. When I asked him, he confirmed his visit to Colorado Springs would occur on January 10. He said he had heard positive things about me from Ken and Wilkens and he looked forward to meeting me when he arrived.

"It'll be a great day for us," he said before ending the call.

The next day I confirmed with Continental Airlines that a reservation had been made for a "Mr. D. Duke" departing from New Orleans Airport to Stapleton International Airport on January 6. A return flight had been confirmed for January 13. I was playing a hunch, and at that time, Continental Airlines was one of the major airline carriers in the country. In that pre-9/11 era doing such a background check was not too difficult for a local police officer, although I did have to jump through a few hoops to eventually acquire the information. It gave me and my colleagues a more definitive answer as to Duke's arrival/departure plans and allowed us to strategize accordingly.

On January 4, in preparation for David Duke's visit to Denver for the nationalization ceremony and the resulting media blitz and anti-Klan community protests that would inevitably follow, a strategy meeting was held at the Denver Police Department. Sergeant Trapp, Jim, and I represented the CSPD.

Representing the Denver Police Department at the strategy planning meeting was their Intelligence sergeant and one of their detectives. A detective from the Lakewood Police Department was also present, as was an investigator from the Colorado Attorney General's Organized Crime Strike Force. It was quickly revealed that one of the unknown attendees at the December 20 meeting between the Klan and the Posse at which *The Birth of a Nation* was shown was the leader of the Posse Comitatus in Lakewood.

I offered the Denver Police Department the opportunity to have a more active role in the investigation by getting one of their Intelligence detectives undercover into the Klan. In that way their officer would be able to monitor activity in the local hate group movement in the same manner that we were doing in Colorado Springs. The Denver sergeant agreed to my offer and said he would have a detective available for our insertion into the group at the upcoming meeting with David Duke.

I had an ulterior motive to my offer to include a Denver undercover officer into the investigation. By doing so I would then have three sets of eyes and ears into the Colorado Klan, and it was my belief that we would—intelligence wise—have the Ku Klux Klan sewn up and perhaps open doors for further penetration into Colorado's hate movement groups. The addition of a third undercover officer was a tremendous move in the right direction and a huge strength to my investigation.

As a result of this meeting, all of these agencies committed a total of seven surveillance officers to provide backup coverage to Chuck and Jim during the nationalization ceremony.

It should be evident that the participation of the Denver and Lakewood police departments and the Colorado attorney general's office demonstrated the seriousness with which law enforcement took the potential risk factors of Duke's presence, the combined Denver and Colorado Klan chapters, and the presence of American Nazi Party, Posse Comitatus, and outlaw motorcycle gang members who also subscribed to white racial supremacist rhetoric and who were expected to attend in celebration of Duke. This was shaping up to be a conclave of the Colorado hate group movement with David Duke as the central figure. To the best of my knowledge, nothing like this had ever happened before in Colorado law enforcement, at least during my employment, and no stone was being left unturned to provide protection to our people. It was also the first time the attorney general's office got involved in the racist hate movement (again, to the best of my knowledge). This was in part because of the Organized Crime Strike Force, dominated and supervised by Denver officers. Other departments throughout the state participated in the strike force as deputized attorney general investigators. Following the conclusion of my KKK investigation I was assigned to the strike force as a narcotics investigator. My supervisor, Robert C. Cantwell, later became chief of the Denver Police Department. When he retired, the governor appointed him to head the Colorado Bureau of Investigation and later the Colorado Department of Corrections.

Now with the extra manpower both on the ground and in the room, I felt ready for Mr. Duke.

By January 6 the media were aware of Duke's imminent visit to Colorado Springs, and the protest groups began to respond accordingly. The *Gazette Telegraph* newspaper reported one such meeting, at noon, in Acacia Park in the heart of the downtown district, involving about twenty people. The anti-Klan protest group involved was People for the Betterment of People. A second group by the name of Citizens for the Reform of Prisoners' Rights showed up in a form of solidarity to publicize their particular cause. They met at the park at the corner of Tejon and Nevada Avenue and marched a few blocks. Walking across the street from them in full view of everyone were two Klansmen countering their protests.

The Denver chapter of the Committee Against Racism (CAR) was scheduled to participate in this demonstration; however, they were unable to make it from Denver.

This demonstration, like others, was a complete failure in the sense that it drew an attendance of only twenty people. For a community that, according to some media reports of the time, was in the throes of outrage over the Klan's presence and Duke's upcoming visit, the presence of only twenty protestors was a paltry number. The group People for the Betterment of People in all likelihood meant well but like other locally formed protests groups lacked true leaders with organizational and rhetorical skills with the capability to rally supporters to a cause. This happened on more than one occasion during this investigation. A small group of citizens expressed their outrage over the Klan's antics yet the overall community response remained tepid.

The two Klansmen who joined the fray by walking the route of the protest were completely ignored by everyone, including the media representatives present. I watched one of them walk up to one of the reporters and ask him if he was looking for a story. When the reporter said yes, the Klansman told the reporter to follow him to his pickup truck. Once there the Klansman put on his robe and the interview began, followed by the march. Other media members observed this and rushed over to the Klansman and stuck microphones and cameras in his face like the maddening rush of paparazzi today. It was a feeding frenzy, a news-making event originating in the actions of the media itself.

The media all too often unwittingly creates the very news it reports because of its zeal to get a story. This only benefits the person or subject being covered and gives them or it a power neither deserves.

On January 7 Chuck and Jim went to an apartment building in Lakewood—the residence of Fred Wilkens—to participate in the nationalization ceremony for formal induction into the Knights of the Ku Klux Klan. Other members from the Colorado Springs chapter were supposed to meet them there; however, when they were escorted to a different room by a member of a Colorado Springs biker gang, they found eleven people present, including some from Colorado Springs. At this time they were formally introduced to David Duke and David Lane, the Klan organizer for the Denver area. They noticed that T-shirts with the inscription WHITE POWER–KU KLUX KLAN were being sold, and they both bought one. They were told that everyone would be going to a local Denny's restaurant for lunch before proceeding to the meeting location. Surveillance units provided backup coverage for the officers throughout this encounter and for the remainder of their stay with Duke.

At the restaurant, Chuck and Jim learned the meeting would

be held at Grange Hall in Wheat Ridge, a city on the north border of Lakewood, 3130 Youngfield Street. Jim slipped away from the group and placed a phone call to the undercover Denver Police detective regarding the location of the meeting. The detective was told to be there so he could be inducted into the Klan. Jim and Chuck then left the restaurant en route to Grange Hall.

By the time they arrived, Ken was there along with the Denver detective. Ken was helping him complete the Klan application form and was being paid the membership dues. With this application, a total of twelve people were going to be nationalized as Klansmen (eight from Colorado Springs and four from Denver, which included one Denver undercover officer). So out of the twelve new members, three were undercover police officers.

The ceremony was approximately sixty minutes long, officiated by David Duke; David Lane, who was the Denver organizer; Ken O'dell; and Joseph Stewart, Ken's second in command. Duke wore his Klan robe, representing his position as the Grand Wizard, and all of the others were also clad in their respective Klan robes. It was a solemn occasion under candlelight that began with the Pledge of Allegiance. Throughout the evening, each presiding official read a portion of the ceremony. Among the first things the inductees had to do was answer "yes" to the following ten questions:

1. *Are you a white, non-Jewish American citizen?*
2. *Is the motive prompting your ambition to be a Klansman sincere and unselfish?*
3. *Have you ever been rejected, upon application, for membership in the Knights of the Ku Klux Klan?*

4. *Do you believe in the Constitution of the United States?*

5. *Are you in favor of a whiteman's government in this country?*

6. *Do you believe in the right of free men to rebel against government tyranny?*

7. *Do you believe in Racial Separation?*

8. *Do you believe in the right for our people to practice the Christian Faith anywhere they assemble, including prayers in schools and public facilities?*

9. *Will you faithfully obey our Klan Constitution and regulations?*

10. *Are you willing to dedicate your life to the protection, preservation, and advancement of the white race?*

At a certain point in the ceremony, the inductees were asked to kneel and pray as Duke sprinkled "holy water" of purification on them and recited the words "In body, In mind, In spirit," resembling the blessing used in the Catholic Church—"In the name of the Father, the Son, and the Holy Spirit." (It is ironic that the KKK would co-opt a section from the Catholic service, a faith that they have historically held in disdain, for one of their most sacred ceremonies. It is one of their many blatant hypocrisies.) That prayer went:

God give us true Whitemen! The Invisible Empire demands
strong minds, great heart, true faith and ready hands.
Men whom the lust of office does not kill;
Men whom the spoils of office cannot buy;
Men whom possess opinions and a will;
Men whom have HONOR; men who will not Lie;
Men who can stand before a demagogue

And damn his treacherous flatteries without winking!
Tall men, sun-crowned, who live above the fog in public
duty and private thinking;
For while the rabble, with their thumb-worn creeds,
Their large professions and their little deeds,
Mingle in selfish, strife, Lo! Freedom weeps
WRONG rules the land, and waiting justice sleeps.
God give us true Whitemen
Men who serve not for selfish booty.
But real men, courageous, who flinch not at duty;
Men of dependable character; men of sterling worth;
Then wrongs will be redressed, and right will rule the earth;
God give us true Whitemen!

At the conclusion of the ceremony the forty people present stayed for a viewing of *The Birth of a Nation*. Chuck noticed that the Posse Comitatus brought a metal detector to the meeting to prevent any visiting attendee from entering the premises carrying a gun. One individual was, in fact, caught with the aid of the device and turned away. Before entering the induction ceremony Chuck and Jim had left their guns in their car. Jim and Chuck posed for a couple of photographs with David Duke. Duke autographed one of them "To Rick Kelley, White Power Forever."

Approximately two weeks later, I received a package in the mail from David Duke's national Klan headquarters in Louisiana. Inside the package was my "Certificate of Citizenship" signed by Duke validating my membership in the Knights of the Ku Klux Klan.

On January 8 Chuck received a call from Ken requesting he go with him to Denver to help provide security for David Duke during his personal appearances. He received word from Fred Wilkens that at one of Duke's appearances there had been about twenty demonstrators shouting anti-Duke and anti-Klan slogans. Ken felt the Klan should respond in kind, and show force in numbers at Duke's next appearance. He said he had already enlisted the aid of several of the Klan's "biker friends" and that if Chuck were to accompany him the next time Duke came under fire it would turn out to be an "ass-kicking match." Chuck told Ken that due to his job he did not think he would be able to make the trip.

On January 9 I telephoned Ken at his residence and told him I heard there was an anti-Klan demonstration planned for Duke's appearance at the KKTV studio in Colorado Springs on January 10 at 6:00 P.M. This demonstration was not a secret; the information was floating in the public sphere, and I was seeking information as to what, if any, response the Klan had planned on Duke's behalf. Ken replied that he wanted a maximum attendance from the local membership tomorrow, but he had failed in his mission to rally one hundred robed members. If they were to march it would be a complete embarrassment for Duke, and the Klan, and so the plan for a rally had been scrapped.

He was going to call the police department to ask for police protection for Duke to help prevent any open display of violence by demonstrators. He then revealed that Duke would have a scheduled luncheon with local membership and the Posse Comitatus at the Bonanza Steakhouse, 1850 N. Academy Boulevard. Following that, Duke would make an appearance on KRDO-TV and at 6:00 P.M. would appear on KKTV to debate a "nigger" professor from the University of Southern Colorado. Ken added he expected Channel 9 News from Denver to also cover Duke's Colorado Springs appearances. Again, the media was fascinated by Duke and the Klan, and willing to give him and their cause the attention and sound bites they so craved.

That same day I received a phone call from one of the protestors I had met at the Acacia Park demonstration. He stated the group he was associated with, Coalition Against Racism and Sexism, had changed its name to the Anti-Racism Coalition (ARC). He said the Denver-based Committee Against Racism (CAR) and the Colorado Springs group People for the Betterment of People would all be gathering downtown at Giuseppe's Depot Restaurant on January 13 and would march to Acacia Park, about a half mile away, for a rally against the Klan. I was invited to attend, and said I'd be there.

About a half hour after my conversation with the protestor, Ken telephoned the night shift commander of the police department and identified himself as the local organizer of the Ku Klux Klan. He explained to the lieutenant that David Duke had three scheduled visits in Colorado Springs the next day and was receiving death threats because of his position as the national leader of the Klan. Ken requested police protection for Duke during his time in the city, between 12:00 P.M. and 8:00 P.M.

The lieutenant told Ken the request would be routed to the proper section within the department. The lieutenant forwarded Ken's request to me in the Intelligence Unit because among our occasional assigned duties was "V-I-P/Dignitary Protection." I passed on the lieutenant's information from Ken to my sergeant and returned my attention to our plans and strategy for Duke's visit the next day. The safety and protection of David Duke was not something I thought I would have to worry about. Little did I know.

9

DUKE OF COLORADO

January 10, the big day everyone had been anticipating since the start of this investigation, had finally arrived. David Ernest Duke, Grand Wizard of the Knights of the Ku Klux Klan, was meeting his entourage of Klansmen at the Bonanza Steakhouse. Their meeting was scheduled for noon; however, early that morning I was summoned to the office of the chief of police.

The chief explained that the department had received several threats against Duke's life during his Colorado Springs visit and did not want anything to happen to him while in "his" city. In the latest twist of fate in this investigation, the chief said he wanted me, Ron Stallworth, official card-carrying "black" member of the Ku Klux Klan, to act as Duke's personal security detail while he was here. Because we had two officers undercover with the Klansmen the chief felt that I alone would be sufficient; if anything of serious consequence broke out the two officers could, out of necessity, break their cover and come to my aid. Meanwhile, the chief had alerted our day shift commander of

Duke's appearances, and the uniformed patrol officers working the particular areas would be extra attentive to those locations and the actions of any anti-Klan demonstrators who might be in the area.

I pleaded with the chief that "placing me in this position could compromise the case because this whole investigation revolved around the Klan's understanding that 'Ron Stallworth' was one of their white members, not a 'black' cop." I pointed out that I could run into somebody during this detail who could reveal my name and thus throw everything into confusion, not to mention the potential risk factor to Chuck and Jim; and Posse Comitatus was part of this entourage and most, if not all, of them would probably be armed.

He understood my concerns but felt the threats were serious enough to warrant this special request; plus there was no one else available at the time, and because of my connection to the case he felt I was the best person under the circumstances.

I was not pleased with the chief's decision. The risk of Chuck's and Jim's undercover identities being compromised in the event a serious incident against Duke happened that warranted my needing their assistance was, in my opinion, too great. I reluctantly left his office with my marching orders to protect the leader of the Klan.

I was to guard Duke not in my uniform but as a plainclothes officer. It would appear to any outside observer that a black man was hanging out with the Klan. Again, I raised objectives to the chief at the ridiculousness of this order, but I loaded my gun with five bullets to kill five assholes if need be and set out for the day.

At the noon meeting at the Bonanza Steakhouse I was surrounded by Klansmen, an uncomfortable moment for most black men, but just another day at the office for me. Present were David Duke, Fred Wilkens, Ken O'dell, Joseph Stewart, Chuck, Jim, and several other local members. Chuck and Jim didn't know that I was guarding Duke until I walked into the restaurant. I gave them a look that said "Everything is okay, don't be alarmed," and we went about our business with barely a nod exchanged between us.

Also present were Posse Comitatus leader Chuck Howarth and several of his membership. Several of them brought their wives to the luncheon. To them, meeting Duke and sharing a meal and a personal moment with him was akin to a patriotic American sharing similar time with the president of the United States. They were literally in awe of Duke's presence, and they basked in what they perceived to be his glory.

Everyone was relaxed as I made contact with Duke. Ken and several of the Klansmen along with Chuck Howarth gathered around to hear what I had to say.

I extended my hand to Duke—addressing him as "Mr. Duke"— which he took and shook in the Klan manner, the index and middle finger extended along the inside wrist while pressing the tips of the fingers into the flesh as the hand is pumped. I later learned this was the Klan's "secret" handshake.

"I am a detective with the Colorado Springs Police Department," I said. I deliberately avoided my name, and got away with it. I was prepared to give one of my undercover names if pressed.

"That's fine. I appreciate the police department's efforts. Thank you," said Duke, still holding my hand.

"I just want you to know that I do not agree with your mission, statements, campaigns, or organization in any way. But I will do my professional duty to see that you get out of my town alive."

"That's fine," he said, releasing my hand.

In an odd way I had a lot in common with Fred Wilkens at that moment. He maintained his job as a firefighter because of his promise to uphold his professional duty to serve and protect the entire population he served, while in his heart he hated so many. That's exactly what I was doing there that day in Colorado Springs, but in reverse. I would have prevented anyone from killing David Duke that day, despite my personal feelings that what he was, and all that he stood for, deserved to be destroyed.

I was a little apprehensive at first about Ken, Fred, and Duke hearing my voice for an extended period, thinking it might trigger something in their memory from our many telephone conversations, but they never recognized it. My apprehension quickly gave way to a renewed sense of confidence that these three individuals and their followers had been completely hoodwinked, bamboozled to the point of incompetence.

I told "Mr. Duke" that we (the CSPD) had received threats against his well-being. I deliberately avoided telling him they were death threats. I told him they were serious enough to warrant my being assigned by the chief of police as his personal security officer during his stay in the city. The PLP was forever threatening Duke, and they were very vocal about taking a fight to the Klan. I was in the unique position of being able to recognize both the Klansmen and the PLP members who desperately wanted to confront the KKK.

I noticed that upon hearing the news that I would be guarding Duke, Fred, Ken, and several others began smiling. I could not tell if they were smiling out of relief that the threats against their leader had been taken seriously to the point of the police department taking official action on his behalf, or if they were smiling at the incongruous spectacle before them: a "nigger" cop being responsible for the personal safety and welfare of their leader, the Grand Wizard of the Knights of the Ku Klux Klan. Whatever their motivation, it brought smiles to their faces. I must confess that I too was chuckling on the inside.

To his credit, Duke was very thankful for the police department's consideration for his well-being and generously expressed his gratitude for the department assuming that responsibility.

That appreciation was echoed by Ken O'dell and Fred Wilkens.

While all of this was taking place, Chuck Howarth merely stood by and glared at me. He was one of my main concerns about having my identity as the "real" Ron Stallworth compromised, because I had previously contacted him on at least two occasions, though I could not recall whether I had ever given him my name or not. As it stood, I believe he recognized me from one of our previous encounters. I was, after all, the only black detective in the department at the time, but he apparently did not remember my name, if he ever knew it, and thus the undercover hoax Chuck, Jim, and I were perpetrating on the Klan remained intact.

I then asked "Mr. Duke" for a favor. He cordially agreed to my request without first asking what it was. I was carrying a Polaroid camera. "Mr. Duke, no one will ever believe me if I tell them I was your bodyguard. Would you mind taking a picture with me?"

He, Wilkens, and Ken smiled at my request and agreed to

pose for a photograph. I then asked Wilkens if he would appear in the photograph with me and Duke, and he also agreed. In the latest display of mockery, I gave the camera to Chuck, the "white" Ron Stallworth, and asked him to take the picture. Both he and Jim could barely contain themselves at my brazen display of contempt at the Klansmen's expense. I had gotten the Grand Wizard and Colorado Grand Dragon/state organizer of the Ku Klux Klan to agree to have their picture taken with me, one of the "niggers" they despised, who in this case was acting as his bodyguard, and the photographer was the undercover officer I had placed in the group whom they all knew as me: Ron Stallworth.

I stood between the two Klan leaders, Wilkens on my left and Duke on my right, and placed my arms around their shoulders. Wilkens thought it was amusing, laughing at my antics and seeing the obvious humor and perhaps publicity propaganda that could be gleaned from such a shot. Duke, however, did not see the humor in my actions. He stepped back while pushing my arm away from his shoulder and said, "I'm sorry, but I can't be seen in a picture with you like that." Wilkens then stopped laughing, but maintained a smile on his face. I replied, "I understand; excuse me for a moment."

I walked over to Chuck, who was still holding the camera, and while pretending to deal with a matter pertaining to the camera, whispered to him, "When you hear me say three, snap the picture." I walked back over to Wilkens and Duke and resumed my position between them except this time my hands were clasped down by my waist. We all smiled for the camera and I counted, "One-two-three."

A fraction of a second before the count of three I raised my hands and once again placed my arms on the right shoulder of Wilkens and the left shoulder of Duke. At that precise moment, Chuck took the picture before Duke could react.

I pulled that stunt in part because no one would ever believe that I was pulling this investigation off. I had the membership card, I had the certificate, but the picture would have been the visual proof of everything, and would have been the real embarrassment for David Duke. Here's a black man cozying up to him. I was determined to get it.

It was a Polaroid, and I've since lost the photo.

Duke immediately bolted from me toward Chuck, as if he had been reacting to the starter's pistol in an Olympic sprint event. I, however, had been a sprinter in school and my reaction time was a split second faster. We both were headed for a common goal: Duke wanted to snatch the camera from Chuck in order to destroy the picture, which he viewed as damaging to his image; I, on the other hand was not going to let him have *my* camera or destroy *my* picture.

Duke reached for the camera in Chuck's hand, but I was a split second faster. He then reached toward me to take it out of my hand and I looked him in the eye with the coldest, most intimidating gaze I could collect and told him, "If you touch me I'll arrest you for assault on a police officer. That's worth about five years in prison. DON'T DO IT!"

Duke stopped dead in his tracks. The smile that had been on the face of Fred Wilkens faded. David Duke glared at me with the most intense look of anger and contempt imaginable and I mischievously smiled at him with the camera in my hand. At this particular moment on this particular issue, the Grand Wizard of the Ku Klux Klan clearly realized that he was a defeated man at the mercy of "something" (not "someone") he hated most—a savage, simian-like in his and the Klan's mind, intellectually inferior "nigger." The difference, though, was in this instance this inferior creature carried a badge and had the force of the law behind him and was willing to use it to make his point. I had no doubt that when Duke backed off from trying to snatch the camera from my hand after hearing my warning, he knew I meant what I said, and so did his followers. I, personally, reveled in his and their mental smack-down.

I looked at that Polaroid developing and thought of my spiritual ancestors over the link of time: black and white, Protestant, Catholic, and Jewish, who had fought and struggled so bravely against the brutality of the Ku Klux Klan over the years. They had lost because they had not been in a position of dominance and control, which is where I currently found myself. I reflected on those involved on the "front lines" of the civil rights struggle: Dr. Martin Luther King Jr. and his primary adviser, Dr. Ralph David Abernathy; Congressman John Lewis of Georgia, who had his skull cracked open by a police officer sympathetic to the Klan, and others who had been subjected to unwarranted arrests based on the Jim Crow laws of the time justifying segregating blacks from whites; physical beatings, sometimes at the hands of police wielding nightsticks; I thought about assault from high-pressure fire hoses and German shepherd police dogs that were employed by Birmingham, Alabama, police commissioner Bull Connor against peaceful, nonviolent civil rights marchers; rape of women, victims of late-night sniper attacks, and bombings. These were scenes I was accustomed to seeing, daily, in my youth on the evening news.

I reflected on April 4, 1968, that day of my freshman year at Austin High School in El Paso, Texas, when the principal announced on the intercom that Dr. King had been killed in Memphis, Tennessee. I remembered the hush that came over the entire school, even as we were dismissed early from classes to go home and avoid the unknown ramifications of what might happen in the aftermath of his death (there were no riots in El Paso). An eerie almost deathly silence enveloped the entire student body of approximately two thousand students as they transitioned from classes to their lockers and then out of the school doors. The primary discernible sound was of girls sobbing and the hushed musings of "I can't believe it" or "Oh my God, what now?" I, along with two of my friends, went to the house of one who had a reel-to-reel tape recording of Dr. King's now famous "I Have a Dream" speech. We sat in the den of his house and listened several times to that sonorous voice that haunts our consciousness to this day echoing, "Free at Last, Free at Last, Thank God Almighty We Are Free at Last!" By the third time we listened to his speech, we all had tears in our eyes at the reality of what had happened to change the course of our collective "black" reality. We also pondered where we, as a people, would be going from here without Dr. King's voice to guide us.

These were the thoughts that ran through my mind in that encounter with David Duke. I felt a sense of connection to those many "strange and bitter fruit," lynched bodies, hanging from the trees over the decades because of the un-God-like atrocities perpetrated on them; and to all of the forgotten others terrorized by the overbearing control and dominance of the Klan and the likes of the David Dukes of generations past. In this instance, however, the positions were reversed. I owned the moment, not the Grand Wizard and his Klan supporters. I held dominion over David Duke, and he clearly did not like it. In essence, he had assumed the role of the "nigger" in this situation and I was his "massa" (master) with a badge and the force of the law to back me up. On a regretful note, that picture was framed but unfortunately buried in a box among a mass of boxes that have accumulated over thirty-five succeeding years and four relocations across the western United States.

Duke continued to glare at me with the most intense look of anger, contempt, and maybe even hatred I had experienced up to that time. I had arrested pimps, prostitutes, and drug dealers and put them in jail and prison for a number of months and/or years who had not spewed the visual bile I received from David Duke. I believe if he could have demonstrated the depth of his humiliation in the form of violence and gotten away with it he would have. Without saying a word, he turned and walked away, followed by Wilkens, Ken, Chuck, Jim, and the rest of his entourage.

The luncheon was held while I sat off to the side observing. Duke made some typical white racial superiority comments to the combined Klan/Posse gathering. I was in view of him and his audience and I did not try to hide my amusement at his claims of white superiority/black inferiority as he and his listeners completely tried to ignore that his claims had been shattered minutes ago by a so-called inferior black. I must note that at no time did he say the pejorative "nigger" in any of his comments because he was putting on his "public" face representative of the "new Klan."

After the luncheon, the group traveled to the KRDO-TV studio, where Duke was interviewed. From there they caravanned to Posse leader Chuck Howarth's house for a "summit" meeting. While they were inside, I sat outside in my car, providing protection.

Duke and Howarth conversed quite freely about their respective groups' activities. Howarth, in particular, eagerly spoke about actions the Posse had recently undertaken; he told Duke that the Posse was behind the recent attempts to recall Colorado Springs mayor Larry Ochs and the charter amendments limiting the powers of the city council, both of which were soundly defeated by the voters. Howarth claimed that because of these efforts his home had been firebombed on two occasions.

Howarth went on to explain to Duke that the Posse Comitatus was a posse in peacetime. At a moment's notice, however, they could "change patches" and become a militia. He said he had a Posse leader in each of the sixty-four counties of the state, thus implying that he was the state leader, which was never verified.

Howarth then went on a racist survivalist rant; he was certain there was going to be a famine soon and those prepared would have to take up arms against those not prepared. Minorities were not preparing themselves for this calamitous event and as a result the white Aryan race would be the ultimate survivors and impose their will on the rest of society. Howarth indicated he had wanted to contact the Klan two years ago when he first saw their newspaper ad but was afraid to act because of his fear that the ad might be a "plant" by the FBI.

While at Howarth's home, Chuck and Jim managed to surreptitiously confiscate Fred Wilkens's copy of *The White Primer: A Dynamic Racial Analysis of Present Day America from the*

Viewpoint of the White Majority. It was reportedly published by a C. W. Bristol. I checked that name through as many police databases—both in-state and out-of-state—as I could at the time and could find nothing on the name. A New Orleans intelligence detective told me C. W. Bristol was a pseudonym used by David Duke, though I was never able to confirm this. The ninety-six-page book was sold by Duke's national offices and it was advertised in the Klan newspaper, *The Crusader.* I later learned *The White Primer* was written by George Lincoln Rockwell, founder of the American Nazi Party.

This is yet another incongruity in the Ku Klux Klan and among most other white supremacist groups. They profess to subscribe to the highest ideals of Americanism—celebrating the U.S. Constitution and hailing the American flag in the process—yet they rank among their pantheon of heroes the likes of Adolf Hitler while singing the praises of the National Socialist movement (Nazi Party) he founded, which led the world to the brink of destruction over sixty years ago. Listed in that pantheon is George Lincoln Rockwell, a decorated American World War II and Korean War Navy commander who founded the American Nazi Party. The KKK salutation is even a reflection of the Nazi influence (a raised right arm, palm down, similar to that of the Nazi salute seen so often in newsreel footage of Nazi soldiers).

The White Primer is Rockwell's manifesto on race relations in America: why blacks are inferior to whites and are, in general, closer on the genetic scale to monkeys, and why Jews are inherently crooked, with blacks acting as their stooges to exploit white providence. Both are responsible for destroying America and bringing down the white race.

When he discovered his copy of *The White Primer* was missing, Fred Wilkens frantically paced the house in search of it, asking people if they had seen it. He never realized that one of his Klansmen, Jim, had slipped it inside his undershirt covered by his shirt and winter jacket, and by the end of the evening's activities the book was in my hands.

At 5:00 P.M., the Klan members made their way to the KRDO radio station for another interview of Duke. In my assigned role as his personal security detail, I accompanied the group to that location in my unmarked police car. Duke, still annoyed with me over my humiliation of him at the earlier luncheon, maintained his silence around me to the point of refusing to acknowledge my presence. Whether he liked it or not, the Grand Wizard for a little while longer had a "nigger" in his life that he could not dominate and control in the finest traditions of the "Old South." I had taken his measure at the luncheon and come out on top, and without his knowledge was still making a fool of him and his organization.

At the conclusion of this radio interview, with his typical philosophical and ideological rant about white supremacy, black inferiority, and Jewish corruption, Duke and his entourage proceeded to the KKTV studio for his debate with the black professor of history from the University of Southern Colorado, located in Pueblo, approximately forty miles south of Colorado Springs.

As we made our way to the television studio I received word from the police dispatcher that an anonymous bomb threat had been phoned in to the studio, threatening Duke's life. The caller also stated that later that evening a meeting would be held at the Northwest Community Center, located at 605 Willamette, to discuss a response to the Klan's growing notoriety in Colorado Springs. As we arrived at the studio there were several anti-Duke/Klan protestors demonstrating at the entrance to the television studio building. They were cursing at Duke and his Klan entourage and a few were flinging small stones at them.

Inside the studio Duke prepared to debate with the black professor about American history, civil rights, and the Klan. For me, standing behind the cameras, the debate was difficult to watch. As a debater, Duke was educated on his side of the issue and extremely articulate in presenting justification for that side. He was always "cool" and polished in his demeanor and seemed to become more so in the face of ad hominem attacks by those not as versed as he. Even when his false claim of facts in support of his racist beliefs were aggressively challenged by his opponents, Duke remained calm and would present a well-reasoned response based on his positional thinking that often left them looking befuddled and him on the low side of brilliant.

That was the state of affairs, as I saw it, with his televised debate with the black professor. Duke seemed to dominate the discussion in spite of the professor's command of historical facts regarding race relations and the Klan's history of white supremacist terrorism. Duke's debate mastery, from my vantage point, completely overwhelmed the professor. In all likelihood, he probably got a measure of vindication from his earlier humiliation at my hands by seeing himself redeemed at the expense of this "academic nigger."

I was saddened to see how shaken the professor was, and angry at how convincingly Duke's forked tongue could spit out the sweetest, most toxic of lies.

After the cameras stopped rolling, we left the studio.

At the conclusion of this debate, Duke's business in Colorado Springs was now over. My role in the visit, helping to secure his safety, was appreciated by Fred Wilkens, who thanked me and shook my hand, but Duke still refused to acknowledge me. Wilkens told me he and Duke were headed back to Denver. I followed his car as far as the nearest on-ramp to Interstate 25 to ensure his safety out of town. My public service as bodyguard to the Grand Wizard was now complete.

10

ROCKY MOUNTAIN FORTRESS

Duke's visit was, for lack of a better word, a success. David Duke had survived, no riots broke out, Ken had bungled (through his own natural ineptitude) a public Klan rally, but also there was no real intelligence learned. Professionally, I felt great. Colorado Springs was successfully protected, there were no cross burnings, and even guarding David Duke was a success. I was proud of the work my team had done.

Personally, I admit there were times I wanted to step aside and allow the crowd outside KKTV to let loose on Duke and Fred and the whole lot. Being there with the KKK was surreal, frightening, and exhilarating all at once. When I look back on the day with David Duke it really feels comical. They had inducted three police officers into the Klan, and had been guarded by a cop who was leading the undercover investigation of them by standing right next to Duke, whom I had spoken to many times.

As funny as it was, I never lost sight of the danger they presented. Had they been on top of their game, like Klansmen in the past, they could have caused serious damage and terror. All of these men had access to weapons, and the day could easily have turned to tragedy. So even though we had survived the visit from David Duke, our work was far from over.

On January 13, the anti-Klan rally was held at Acacia Park. This was the same demonstration I had been invited to on January 9 and again on January 11. Since then I had spoken with Ken on the phone and learned that he planned to be there, as he put it, "undercover," wearing his Klan robe, so he could take pictures of the protest speakers, in particular those from Denver.

I was there in an undercover capacity, plainclothed, monitoring the situation.

Ken arrived at the park shortly after noon, took about six pictures, and then made his way to his pickup truck. At this point a new obstacle appeared, confounding my efforts to control this investigation.

Though we in the Intelligence Unit had tried to keep as much of a lid on the investigation as possible, it was inevitable that the more people who knew about it, the greater the risk that word would eventually spread about our conducting a unique undercover operation. Virtually the entire Colorado Springs criminal justice system knew about this "crazy black cop" who was pulling a sting on the KKK and had gained membership into the group.

One of my colleagues who had heard about the investigation was Officer Ed. Under the department's command structure, Vice and Intelligence were supervised by the same sergeant; therefore, Officer Ed and I both answered to Sergeant Trapp. That was where our similarities ended because his job was to focus on the vice activities within the city and nothing more. On the day of the Acacia Park rally, however, he had been sent with me to monitor the demonstration, in essence acting as my backup, and nothing more. He chose, however, to take that simple assignment and go much further with it, providing me with cause for concern and forcing me later to take the matter to Sergeant Trapp.

Officer Ed saw Ken at the park and took it upon himself to go up and introduce himself. He told Ken that he had been following his movements in the paper and thought he and the Klan were doing the right thing. Officer Ed further told Ken that he felt the protestors were "full of shit," and that he was interested in talking to him further. He requested Klan literature because he was interested in joining the group.

Ken was receptive to Officer Ed's overture, telling him that he was glad to hear him say that about the protestors and he wished more people shared the same point of view.

By this time, Ken, who was accompanied by Tim, noticed that several protestors recognized him, and the two of them hurriedly got in his truck, preparing to leave the area. Before doing so, Ken gave Officer Ed a Klan business card and told him to write to the address on the card with a request for literature and it would be sent to him.

Officer Ed essentially did what I had done three months earlier to get the investigation under way—which he was aware of—except he, by virtue of being a white officer, was able to have a face-to-face contact with Ken rather than a telephone conversation. As for the literature he was requesting from Ken, I had all of the Klan literature we wanted or needed, including a subscription to their newspaper, *The Crusader*. Officer Ed had accomplished nothing of any consequence except to inject himself into an investigation that did not need or want his presence. I already had two undercover officers—Chuck and Jim—available for any face-to-face contact necessary and saw no need to oversee a third officer. Officer Ed's efforts were literally two months behind the curve.

Some of the protestors closed in on the truck as Ken pulled away from Officer Ed. As he did, Tim undid his jacket to reveal a Ku Klux Klan T-shirt, put a ski mask with eye openings on his face, and raised his right fist to the closing demonstrators as the truck sped down the street. The truck stopped at an intersection, and sitting alongside it was a KKTV news vehicle. Ken yelled to the occupants, "Do you want an interview?"

The journalists, again demonstrating complicity in promoting the Klan's efforts, followed Ken's truck a couple of blocks farther, the two vehicles stopped, and the occupants made contact with one another. The media interviewed Ken for five minutes and then everyone left the area. Ken's interview was aired on the ten o'clock news that evening.

I took up the matter of Officer Ed's indiscretion with Sergeant Trapp, who told him to stick to his area of assignment and stay out of my investigation unless otherwise instructed. Officer Ed's insistence on injecting himself into the case was to become a recurring nightmare to me.

Meanwhile, the rally at Acacia Park drew a crowd estimated at a hundred, a number the Klan had failed to gather for themselves. Douglas Vaughn addressed the crowd and told them he was a member of the Progressive Labor Party. He handed out various INCAR leaflets to the crowd as well as two-by-fours with placards attached, bearing anti-Klan slogans. He carried a bullhorn in one hand and a baseball bat to crack open heads in the other as he led the demonstrators in various chants:

Ku Klux Klan, Scum of the Land
and
Duke, Duke, Duke the Puke

Doug asked me several times to address the crowd, but I feigned a reserved shyness about speaking before an unknown group of people and declined each time. The demonstration drew together a wide array of community activist groups based in Colorado Springs and Denver, including:

La Mecha (Colorado College in Colorado Springs)
Black Student Union (Colorado College in Colorado Springs)
La Raza (Colorado Springs)
Anti-Racist Coalition (Colorado Springs)
People for the Betterment of People (Colorado Springs)
Gay Coalition (Denver)
PLP/INCAR (Denver)
Colorado Workers United Council (Denver)

Marianne Gilbert of INCAR introduced me to her husband, Alan. She invited me to attend a meeting that evening at a Colorado Springs residence to discuss the formation of an INCAR chapter in Colorado Springs. She also introduced me to a black Fort Carson soldier and his wife who she said was in charge of organizing Fort Carson military personnel on behalf of INCAR.

I declined to attend the meeting that evening because of the lack of time to properly prepare for backup surveillance contingencies and other issues.

The general attitude of the crowd was peaceful and nonviolent with the exception of Doug Vaughn and the INCAR people, who openly advocated a violent confrontation with the Klan and, if necessary, the police. A representative of the Black Student Union of Colorado College, during his address to the crowd, said, "If the police do not stop the Klan then the only recourse is to rely on the masses to prevent the spread of the Klan's message of hate."

At the end of the speeches, the crowd marched the three to four blocks to the Judicial Complex, where the demonstration disbanded.

Prior to leaving the park, Marianne, Alan, and Doug once again invited me to attend a dinner meeting later that night to discuss the formation of a Colorado Springs INCAR chapter. I, once again, declined, but left the door open for a later date.

My hesitation in joining them was because I needed to obtain more intelligence on the background of these three individuals before walking into their personal domain, especially someone with as volatile a personality as Doug with his open advocacy of violent, armed confrontation with the police. Another representative from the Anti-Racist Coalition (ARC) also invited me to his residence to further discuss action against the Klan. This offer too was declined for the moment.

On January 14 I decided it was time to have a conversation with David Duke following his Colorado Springs appearance four days earlier. I wanted to assess his reaction to his visit and everything that transpired. I placed the call to the Klan national office in Louisiana.

"This is Ron Stallworth, in Colorado Springs."

"Oh, hi. How are you?" As ever, Duke was friendly and warm.

"Meeting you was so empowering—really made me want to know more, and become a better Klansman," I said.

I told him how honored I was to finally meet him in person. He reciprocated in response.

I expressed my regret that I did not have the opportunity to spend some one-on-one time with him because I wanted to soak up more of his knowledge and wisdom about being a Klansman.

Duke expressed regret that his busy schedule during his time in Colorado prevented him from getting to know the local membership on a more personal basis. He said he accomplished a lot though in terms of his talks with Posse leader Chuck Howarth, though he did not reveal any specifics.

"I have to ask, Mr. Duke. Did anything surprise you about your visit?" I said. I wanted to see if he had any suspicions about me, or the "Ron Stallworth" he thought he knew.

His response very nearly brought me to tears from laughter. He proceeded to tell me about his encounter with the, as he put it, "nigger cop who threatened to arrest me for assaulting him." Obviously, I wanted to see if he had any suspicions about the black cop who was assigned to guard him.

Duke told me the story of that encounter as if I (Chuck) had not been there. The incident still clearly bothered him, as he commented on the problem with giving minorities positions of authority that they use, as he put it, to take advantage of whites. I responded by telling Duke that the "nigger cop, under a different circumstance, would be taught a serious lesson for the way he acted toward you."

Duke agreed with my assessment. His final comment on the subject was that his encounter with that "nigger" was the only negative aspect of his Colorado trip. He added that he did not consider the demonstrators against him and the Klan to be much of a problem compared to the "nigger cop" because he was accustomed to and expected to be demonstrated against wherever he went to rally Klan troops.

We then discussed upcoming Klan events in which he was going to be involved. He told me about Klan rallies planned for Los Angeles and Kansas City in the next few weeks. They were expecting strong resistance from protest groups but would maintain a nonviolent stance until provoked. And, he emphasized, this applied to the police as well. Our conversation ended shortly thereafter and I immediately contacted police departments in those cities to inform them of Duke's rally plans.

In the late morning of January 14 I was visited at my office by two agents of the Peterson Air Force Base Office of Special Investigations (OSI). They said they had heard about my "interesting" investigation involving military personnel and were interested in learning more about who might have a connection with the Air Force.

I asked them how they knew about the investigation, since I had not openly discussed the undercover aspect of it with anyone except those with an absolute need to know. I had not even discussed the investigation with the Fort Carson military police (MP) or their investigative arm, the Criminal Investigation Detachment (CID).

While I was working in the Narcotics section (1975 to 1977), there was one military police unit that had a reputation for being untrustworthy. They would sell drugs, commit burglaries, armed robberies, and sexual assaults. They were dirty. Our officers—uniformed and detectives—had made numerous cases against members of this particular MP unit for a variety of criminal offenses including drugs and burglary. We did not trust anyone assigned to this particular group and carried that feeling over to the entire MP command on Fort Carson. In terms of CID, we, in Narcotics, worked very closely with their commander, a chief warrant officer at the time; however, his complement of investigators came from the ranks of the military police. This was the dilemma I faced in terms of communicating with the Army. Their CID commander knew the CSPD Intelligence Unit had an open file on the Ku Klux Klan but had never been told, by me, that we were operating an undercover "sting." If he or any military personnel, including the Air Force, knew about that aspect of the investigation, they would have had to learn it from one of my superiors or from someone else in the department with both knowledge and loose lips, and there were many.

The OSI agents did, in fact, tell me that one of my superiors discussed the investigation with one of their superiors, including its undercover aspect. They then asked me specifics about how it unfolded.

After I told them the story and got the usual laughter at the hoax we were pulling on the Klan, the OSI agents got serious. They asked if they could see my investigation casebook and the list of names of those Klan members with a military connection. I produced the book, opened it to the page in question, and showed it to them. One of them ran his index finger down the list of names and then stopped. He looked up at me and asked if I could take a ride with them. I asked where we would be going, but he refused to say. He asked again if I could take a ride with them. I asked a second time and got the same response.

By this time, my interest in their interest in my list of names was piqued. I was curious about their dire need for secrecy and the location they wanted to take me to. I looked over at Sergeant Trapp for counsel as to what I should do. He too was curious by their intense desire to keep the location of the intended destination a secret. Ultimately, Sergeant Trapp left the decision to go up to me.

After a couple of minutes of contemplation (after all, who completely trusts the federal government, especially the military?), I finally agreed to accompany the OSI agents to go "wherever." They were pleased with my decision and asked if I would bring my investigation casebook. I grabbed the book and asked the two agents for their business cards. I gave their cards to Sergeant Trapp and told him that if my body failed to turn up in a respectable amount of time, then start the investigation with these two agents. I got in their car and we drove away, making our way onto the southbound on-ramp of Interstate 25.

I asked a third time where we were going and received only silence in response. The reason for their secrecy did not become clear until we approached the exit sign that read NORAD and the car veered right toward Cheyenne Mountain, site of the joint U.S.-Canadian North American Aerospace Defense Command. At this realization and the sight of the twenty-five-ton blast doors that protect the main entrance to the tunnel of the hollowed-out mountain complex, I began smiling like a kid in a candy store. (In those days—I cannot speak for today—

officers at my level did not get into NORAD. It was and still is a top security clearance facility.) As we drove through the security checkpoint, my mind flashed back to the first time I had ever heard the name NORAD.

It was Christmas Eve, 1963. I was a ten-year-old living in El Paso, Texas, on East Yandell Street, attending Alta Vista Elementary School. It was around 9:00 P.M. and on the radio program my mother was listening to I heard the announcer mention that NORAD had spotted Santa's sleigh flying over a particular location in the eastern North American sky, making his rounds delivering gifts to children. The radio announcer said NORAD would be tracking Santa's sleigh throughout the night, and if you looked up into the evening sky you might catch a glimpse of his sleigh as a result of moonlight shimmering off its rails and undercarriage. I even remember him saying that if you saw such a sight to look closely because you might catch a quick glimpse of Rudolph's red nose shining brightly in the night sky.

My younger brother and I ran outside and began scanning the sky, looking in different directions, hoping to catch sight of that shimmering sleigh and the bright shining red nose of Rudolph. I was a Cub Scout and knew how to locate the Big Dipper, the Little Dipper, and the North Star, but finding Santa's sleigh being led by Rudolph with his "nose so bright" proved fruitless. We gave up, went back inside the house, and about an hour later went to bed. When I woke up the next morning I found that the shimmering sleigh NORAD had reported on the night before had, in fact, found its way to 3308 E. Yandell Street.

The OSI agents drove inside the tunnel. Day suddenly turned to night. There was a two-lane road with a yellow stripe down the center, and the darkness inside the mountain was illuminated by lights as if we were driving at night. I did not know how far inside the mountain the road went, but the lights seemed to go on forever, or it could have been an optical illusion elevated by my mind playing tricks on me from being awestruck at this formidable military installation.

To the right of the entry point were fifteen three-story buildings sitting on top of giant springs that were designed to allow the buildings to shift up to an inch in any direction in case of explosion or an earthquake. (NORAD was built in the midst of the cold war with the former Soviet Union and designed to withstand a nuclear attack.) In essence, NORAD is a city inside a mountain employing six hundred people, with a small store, cafeteria, gym, medical center, and more.

This was all explained to me by a deputy commander at the facility, a black colonel, who was introduced to me by one of the OSI agents after we made our way into one of the many buildings. The colonel said he had heard about my "unique" investigation and wanted to know more about it.

I told him the story and showed him my KKK membership card. He was a son of the South and got a good laugh out of that and my tale about the camera confrontation with David Duke. The colonel then got serious and asked to see my investigation casebook with its list of military names of Klan members.

I opened the book to the list of names, and like the OSI agents did in my office, the colonel scrolled his index finger down the list. He suddenly stopped, picked up the phone, and dialed a number. He turned his back to me and the agents as he spoke in a hushed tone to whoever was on the other end of the line and then hung up. The colonel then turned his attention back to me, made small talk for a few moments, congratulated me on the success of my "sting" of the Klan and service as a police officer, shook my hand, and then left the room after speaking privately with the two OSI agents.

"Okay, what is going on?" I asked.

The OSI agents stated that two of the names on my list, which were never identified to me, were NORAD personnel with top-security-clearance-level status. Their job was to man the main console monitoring North America's air defense systems mechanism. The agents explained that the phone call made by the colonel was to the Pentagon, where he received permission to transfer the two Klansmen from their top secret position.

The agents indicated the Pentagon viewed their activity as having potential national security implications and that individuals such as these two would not be tolerated. According to the OSI agents, the two Klansmen would be transferred by the end of the day to the "North Pole," the farthest northern military installation in the U.S. command. The agents said the colonel was adamant that the behavioral attitude and activities exhibited by these two Klansmen and any other NORAD personnel with similar tastes was unacceptable.

The colonel thanked me for my time and left the room. The two agents I was with nodded at me, and we walked out of the building inside the mountain and got back in our car. With that, my visit to the location that tracked Santa's sleigh on its Christmas trek across the North American continent during my childhood came to an end.

11

UP IN SMOKE

Chuck and Sergeant Trapp couldn't believe my NORAD story, and it only served to give me an extra bounce in my step. My investigation had reached the top echelons of the U.S. government, and taken down white supremacists who had some of the highest clearances in the U.S. military. Not bad for a young cop.

In the days after my time inside the mountain, I had three separate phone conversations with Ken regarding cross burnings.

During those three conversations Ken invited me to accompany him and other Klansmen to specific locations to ignite eighteen-foot crosses using the matchbook-cigarette method he got off a James Bond movie. Ken told me the date, time, and other details, such as how many members would be participating in the cross-burning ceremony. When I learned such information I would notify the CSPD Uniformed Patrol Division shift commander and request that extra patrol cars be assigned to the specific areas in question to either catch the Klansmen in the act or provide enough of an intimidating factor to prevent them from going through with it in the first place.

In an era before cell phones and the blessings of instant communication via text messaging and email, I would have to wait at least twenty-four hours before I learned if my department's response efforts worked.

When I finally did speak with Ken I begged off participating because of other binding obligations, but the real reason was the legal issue of entrapment. He told me they had to cancel their burn because multiple police cars were near the cross-burning site; one site had three patrol cars in an area that typically had only one and an occasional one-hour overlap of two, crisscrossing up and down streets near or at the site. This exhibit of a strong police presence on those two occasions prompted the Klan to cancel their cross-burning plans and ultimately to completely disregard the third one. It was a proud moment to be a police officer!

I have often been asked, "What did you really accomplish over the course of this investigation without arresting any Klan members or seizing any illegal contraband?" or "What are you most proud of where this investigative effort was concerned?" My answer is always in this fashion: "As a result of our combined effort, *no* parent of a black or other minority child, or any child for that matter, had to explain why an eighteen-foot cross was seen burning at this or that location—especially those individuals from the South who, perhaps as children, had experienced the terrorist act of a Klan cross burning. No child in the city limits of Colorado Springs ever had to experience firsthand the fear brought on by this act of terror. We prevented them from having such an incident burned into their consciousness, as many of their parents might have been imprinted as children. I knew firsthand from direct dealings via my undercover phone conversations with Ken when and where those acts of terror were being planned, and we in the police department were able to put a stop to them. Success in a police investigation does not always rest on how many arrests are made or how much illegal contraband is seized." Success often lies not in what happens but in what you prevent from happening.

Officer Ed, in his self-serving zeal to establish a name for himself and advance his career, thought he was providing me with a valuable contribution to the investigation with the information Ken had revealed to him. Officer Ed's attempt to join the Klan was nothing more than a self-ingratiating effort on his part to try to impress me and Sergeant Trapp and secure for himself a transfer from Vice into the Intelligence Unit. His actions were not in the best interest of my investigation and I was not pleased, to say the least.

With the Duke visit past us, and Ken's reluctance to continue any plans for burnings, I started to wind down the undercover aspect of the Klan investigation. Chuck and Jim were more heavily engaged in their Narcotics assignment, and their job priorities had to take precedence over mine. Their lieutenant, Arthur, still held a strong dislike for me, and I did for him, and in terms of intelligence gathering we were not developing much new information on the group. I was still trying to identify the local membership and monitoring their activities via phone calls to and from Ken, but face-to-face meetings using Chuck and Jim had stopped by this time.

In addition to my continued phone calls to Ken, I was also still having telephone contact with Fred Wilkens and David

Duke, though much less frequently and not really discussing much of serious consequence. Those calls, more than anything else, were for the purpose of keeping a line of communication open between me and them. One notable incident did happen, however, that allowed me another brush with a historic figure from the civil rights movement of my youth.

On March 29, 1979, Dr. Ralph David Abernathy, the man who was arguably the right-hand man to Dr. Martin Luther King Jr. and succeeded him at the helm of the Southern Christian Leadership Conference, arguably the primary group behind the civil rights movement, visited Colorado Springs. At virtually every physical conflict faced by Dr. King, Dr. Abernathy was at his side, suffering the same pain and indignity. His visit, sponsored by a black Baptist church cofounded by my late aunt in Fountain, Colorado, a small city located ten miles south of Colorado Springs and just east of Fort Carson, was a public relations opportunity for the church. A fifteen-year-old black boy, David Scott Lee, had recently been convicted in Colorado Springs for murdering a young adult white male cook at a twenty-four-hour downtown diner. The cook, married with a young daughter, was on his way home from working a graveyard shift when Lee pulled up alongside him and shot him dead. When questioned about why he had committed the crime, the teenager said he just wanted to know what it felt like to kill someone.

The district attorney charged Lee with murder in adult court and this earned him the wrath of the black minister and congregation of the Baptist church. A protest movement started on behalf of the young murderer, accusing the district attorney of being a racist for prosecuting Lee in adult court rather than in the juvenile court, where his sentence would have been lighter.

They completely ignored the cold-blooded nature of his crime or the aftereffect of his actions on the young widow and her now fatherless daughter. In their mind, the true victim was the fifteen-year-old murderer who wanted to see what it felt like to kill someone and did it.

The Baptist church convinced Dr. Abernathy to come to Colorado Springs to add "star power"—his name and status—to their protest effort against the district attorney. Their whole argument was based on the race of the two principal parties and was that the murderer had not been treated fairly by the criminal justice system by being charged as an adult—because he was black.

On that same date, approximately twenty-five Klan members—some wearing their robes and others wearing KKK WHITE POWER T-shirts—picketed the Baptist church while Dr. Abernathy preached a sermon in support of the protest effort. Some of the Klan members present included Fred Wilkens, Joseph Stewart, and Tim.

I was at the church because earlier I had been contacted by my chief, who told me about death threats being received by the department against Dr. Abernathy, allegedly made by Klan members. The chief told me I was to stay with Dr. Abernathy as his personal security (bodyguard) until he left town later in the evening. (Note: I'd gone from being the bodyguard of the Grand Wizard of the Ku Klux Klan in January, to the bodyguard three months later of the leader of the civil rights movement the Klan worked so vehemently against.)

Following the church service, I introduced myself to Dr. Abernathy (which was a great honor) and explained my purpose for being there. He was very polite, very gracious, a genuine southern gentleman (it is interesting to note that he was one of my late mother-in-law's professors at Alabama State University, though I did not know that at the time). He thanked me for my time and concern for his welfare and seemed most appreciative.

Members of the church congregation, however, were just the opposite. As I was talking to Dr. Abernathy, I overheard the minister whispering derogatorily to some of his congregation that I must think I'm *Starsky & Hutch*, referring to the popular television cop show of the time and specifically commenting on my dress (jeans, casual shirt and sneakers, similar to that of the TV characters but typical of my day-to-day attire). The social climate of the time was such that these church members did not trust any criminal justice official. They resented my presence among them with Dr. Abernathy and clearly did not want any police officer intruding on his visit with them and their cause.

The church congregation was planning a protest demonstration later that day at the downtown Colorado Springs courthouse, where the district attorney's office was located. In the interim, Dr. Abernathy was driven to his hotel to relax until the demonstration. I stayed in the room with him and for the next two to three hours I had a talk with a piece of living history of the civil rights movement. I was so awestruck about seeing this man I had seen so many times on the news, in papers, and on television. I was amazed that I had been assigned to make sure this civil rights icon was safe. It was an honor.

Although he was tired (he removed his shoes and stretched out on the love seat), he kindly answered my questions about his experiences in the civil rights movement, and his remembrance of Dr. King, and of being the victim of KKK terrorism tactics. He was a black child of the South of his time and had grown up under the ever-present threat of death or some manner of retribution from racially centered white men, some clad in white hooded robes. He had been the victim of a bombing and been present when his best friend and closest ally in the civil rights movement—Dr. King—had been shot and killed on that motel balcony in Memphis, Tennessee. This was a man who was no stranger to death and who did not cower in the face of threats from white-robed, hooded terrorists.

To say I was awestruck by being able to share this private time with him and hear him speak of his experiences in the movement that, for me, was merely images on a television screen's nightly news report, would be an understatement. Without meaning to sound belittling to Dr. Abernathy, who was an extremely accomplished man in his own right, as I sat there soaking up the living history of my youth from one of the persons who shaped it, I felt honored; yet I couldn't help but think that by sharing this moment with him I was vicariously experiencing a bit of Dr. King himself. In essence, I was channeling Dr. King through Dr. Abernathy, who had shared virtually every adult-life experience with him since the 1955–56 Montgomery, Alabama, bus boycott, the seminal event of the civil rights movement.

During a pause in his recollections, I asked Dr. Abernathy if he knew the story behind the protest effort being put on by his church sponsors against the district attorney. He said he had been told the district attorney had falsely charged a fifteen-year-old black boy with murdering a white man and had sought to treat the child more harshly than he normally would a white child if he had committed a similar crime.

I then chose to break professional protocol by doing something that a person serving on a VIP protection detail is not supposed to do: I got personally involved in the business of my professional assignment. Dr. Abernathy had been lied to by his church sponsors, and I felt a sense of duty to tell this honest, good, decent, historical treasure to the black community the truth.

I proceeded to tell him about the intimate details of the case that the minister and church members had conveniently chosen to leave out of the narrative. He perked up at my mention of the family nature of the white murder victim, an innocent young man with no prior knowledge of his fifteen-year-old killer. He displayed surprise and anger at learning the reason behind the killing—the teenager merely wanted to see what it felt like to kill someone and chose this particular victim at random. I told Dr. Abernathy that his confession had been voluntarily given and he had never retracted it. I also emphasized to him that his victim could just as easily have been a person of color, at which point would the church be holding the same grievance against the district attorney over the victim's race?

I finally said to Dr. Abernathy that this poor victim was a hardworking man just trying to provide for his young family in a hot, dirty, low-paying job, who became a random choice of a young, sick kid's desire to experience bloodlust. Race was not a motivating factor in any aspect of this case other than the random coming together of the two principal parties.

When Dr. Abernathy heard this revelation, his face took on a marked change of expression. I could see confusion and a hint of anger in his eyes. I believe he now realized that he had been duped by his church sponsors, that everything had been a ruse to attach his name to their personal vendetta against the district attorney. I think he was trying to figure out how, having come this far, with all the publicity that had been attached to his presence with the minister and his congregation over this issue, he could possibly back out now. His body language changed from one of relaxed stretching on the love seat to sitting in an upright, very attentive position. His only comment to me was, "That does change things quite a bit now, doesn't it?" I replied, "I would think so, sir; at least it would for me."

At about this time the minister returned to the room to pick up Dr. Abernathy and take him to the courthouse for the demonstration. I sat and watched as the two of them stood face-to-face, engaged in what appeared to be a very heated discussion. They were speaking in hushed tones, so I could not overhear what was being said, but their body language was very revealing. Dr. Abernathy's hands were chopping the air as he spoke and I noticed he turned several times looking my way as a hand chop was directed at me. The minister, on the other hand, was clearly playing defense, trying to calm him down while occasionally looking in my direction with the spirit of the Lord clearly not in him.

Did what I say to Dr. Abernathy matter? Had it changed his opinion about his mission during this Colorado Springs visit? I will never fully know the answers to those questions because the matter was not mentioned to me ever again and never discussed by the minister for the remainder of his visit or after he left. The minister knew me through my aunt, the cofounder of his church. My aunt did not speak to me for a period of time after I told her that her church lied to Dr. Abernathy and the whole protest effort was nothing more than a sham using his name for publicity purposes.

After their animated discussion, Dr. Abernathy pulled

himself together while the minister gave me a most bitter look, and the three of us left the hotel room and proceeded to the courthouse courtyard where the demonstration would take place. Greeting us were a group of about twenty-five Klan members, some in their white robes and some in their KKK WHITE POWER T-shirts, who were already assembled and marching in a circle carrying two-by-fours with placards attached bearing written slogans denouncing the church demonstrators, and expressing support for the decision to prosecute the fifteen-year-old murderer as an adult.

Dr. Abernathy and the church minister joined members of the congregation, my aunt included, and they began their version of a counterprotest. They did not carry placards with slogans but rather shouted phrases denouncing the district attorney's actions while keeping with the black tradition in civil protest efforts of singing Negro (black) spirituals. They all seemed to revel in the moment when Dr. Abernathy led them in the singing of the theme song of the civil rights movement, "We Shall Overcome." The years seemed to fall from their faces and shoulders as they all, with the grace of one of the primary leaders of the civil rights movement among them, stood in a circle (as many of them had seen done so often on their TV screens in that bygone period with this man at the helm along with his good friend, Dr. King) and locked hands and while swaying from side to side sang:

We shall overcome, we shall overcome We shall overcome
someday, someday Deep in my heart, I do believe
We shall overcome, someday . . .

I stood off to the side and watched what I considered to be a "clown" show. The most clownish part of this show was watching my aunt, the church minister, and other members of the congregation running their "con" on a venerable figure of our collective cultural history as black people. He deserved better. They seemed to be basking in the glow of participating in a protest demonstration with a man of Dr. Abernathy's stature, someone who had shed blood for the cause of civil rights for all Americans. They wanted to live a part of that struggle through his presence and participation in their faux crisis of racial injustice.

David Scott Lee, the fifteen-year-old murderer convicted as an adult, was sentenced to life in the Colorado State Penitentiary.

The next day, March 30, I received a phone call from Ken on the undercover line. He told me once again, and this time very adamantly, that I needed to assume leadership of the local Klan chapter because of his and Joseph Stewart's impending departure from Colorado Springs resulting from their discharge from the Army. He said the chapter needed a steady hand, a level head, and a local resident to lead it, not a military man who would be coming and going as duty called. That did not make for a stable situation, and what the chapter needed was stability. That's what my assuming the local organizer role would do, bring stability to the leadership of the Colorado Springs Klan chapter. He said the membership had previously decided that I was the one best suited for the role, and he insisted that I meet with him to set the leadership transition in motion.

I tried once more to talk Ken out of this notion of me assuming the role of local organizer of the Klan, using different tactics.

I tried the humble routine that I wasn't worthy of such an honor, and offered my job as being an impediment, but his response was that it could be worked out. I then suggested others better suited for the position, which he rejected outright. Every reason, every excuse I gave Ken as to why I could not become the leader of the Colorado Springs Ku Klux Klan he shot down. He ended our conversation by stating he would call me back in a couple of days to set up a meeting to finalize a leadership transition.

I immediately notified Sergeant Trapp of this development, and he suggested we discuss it with the chief of police.

When we met with the chief, I presented a summary of the entire investigation: (1) the valuable intelligence that had been gathered on two of our most extreme racial hate groups (the Klan and Posse Comitatus); (2) the discovery of their infiltration of our military installations (U.S. Army and Air Force/ NORAD); (3) prevention of black militant groups (Black Panther Party and Black Muslims) from coming to Colorado Springs and merging their verbal venom with the Klan's, thereby negatively affecting our community social dynamic; (4) the prevention, on at least two occasions, of the terroristic acts of Klan cross burnings; and (5) the national impact we were having from an intelligence standpoint that was proving beneficial to police agencies and private entities (e.g., the ADL) throughout the country.

I then informed the chief of my earlier conversation with Ken and his adamant insistence that I assume the leadership role of the local Klan chapter. I lobbied the chief in favor of accepting Ken's offer because: (1) We, the department, could work around any potential entrapment issues that might come up by working in close consultation with the district attorney's office; and (2) the window of opportunity being presented to us to gather intelligence on the Klan and, by extension, others in the Colorado hate group movement—from a position of leadership—was an unprecedented, once-in-a-lifetime opportunity that we should take advantage of while we had the chance.

Sergeant Trapp listened to my argument, was in favor of proceeding with the investigation, and fully supported my positions.

The chief, however, would not bend to the logic of my reasoning and, in fact, did not even want to discuss the issue.

His position was for me to immediately shut down the investigation. I was ordered to cease any further contact with Ken and to have no further face-to-face meetings with any Klan members. Sergeant Trapp was ordered to have the undercover phone line changed so no further calls from Ken could come to me, and I was not to respond to any mail that might be sent by the Klan to the undercover P.O. box address. The chief made it clear that he wanted "Ron Stallworth—Klansman" to completely disappear.

I've often been asked why he not only wanted the investigation to stop, but also wanted it to be expunged from the record. I can't answer exactly why, because I do not know what was in his heart and mind, but he was in charge of public relations.

I believe he was fearful that if word got out that CSPD officers were sworn Klansmen he would have a PR disaster on his hands.

This was an intelligence investigation, not a criminal investigation resulting in no charges.

I questioned the chief as to why he wanted to take this

approach. He explained that he wanted no indication that a "Ron Stallworth—Klansman" ever existed, and that applied to Detective Jim Rose as well. To this end, the chief told me to destroy all evidence that existed that showed the Colorado Springs Police Department had been conducting an undercover investigation into the Ku Klux Klan. He did not want the public to ever know that the CSPD had undercover officers who were Klan members.

I argued vehemently against the chief's logic, with Sergeant Trapp tapping me several times on my knee out of the chief's line of sight, trying to calm me down. I explained that everything I—we—had accomplished was within the moral, ethical, and legal grounds of the law, as well as within departmental policy guidelines. I also reminded the chief that everything was done with Sergeant Trapp's knowledge and his authorization. I argued that taking the steps the chief was advocating implied that we in the Intelligence Unit had done something wrong when, in fact, we had not.

As I said before, the chief, who had been the lieutenant in charge of the public relations section of the police department prior to his elevation in rank, was very conscious of his and the department's public image. He felt it would be detrimental to that image if the citizens of Colorado Springs were made aware of their department's involvement with the Ku Klux Klan, regardless of whether that involvement was officially sanctioned or not. He was adamant that he wanted *all* evidence of our involvement with the Klan destroyed, including *all* of the reports that were generated by the officers involved.

I reluctantly surrendered to the chief's directive and angrily returned to my office with Sergeant Trapp, muttering every curse word in my vocabulary and inventing a few new ones along the way. His most definitive statement regarding the chief's directive was, "Son of a bitch, that's not right." Nearly a year's worth of very innovative, valuable hard work was about to be flushed down the toilet because of the chief's timidity in the face of "possible" public reaction to finding out about what we had been doing. From my perspective, based on the public's response in protesting the Klan's presence, I felt if they found out what their police department had been doing behind the scenes, how we had been making fools out of the Klan all these months, they would have loved it, applauded our effort, and it would have been a public relations coup for the department.

In Sergeant Trapp's presence, I slowly began shredding a report here and a report there (not very meaningful ones). As I was going about this business, the undercover phone line rang several times. Because I had been ordered not to have any further contact with Ken, I did not bother to answer the phone (that was in the days before caller ID, so I had no idea who might be calling). When Sergeant Trapp left the office for an extended period of time I grabbed the investigative casebook and a few other articles accumulated during the course of the investigation, tucked them under my arms, and walked out of the office to my car and drove home. I've kept them with me throughout my travels over the past thirty-five years and they were the basis on which this book was written.

How do I explain my actions? The chief ordered me to "destroy" *all* evidence of the investigation that showed signs of CSPD involvement. He did not, however, tell me "how" to destroy that evidence. By taking it home, all signs of CSPD involvement were removed from CSPD files, as the chief wanted.

Did I ever lie about what I did? No, because no one ever asked if I had destroyed the evidence as the chief had ordered, so I was never put in the position of having to decide how to answer that question.

Had knowledge of my actions been made known to Sergeant Trapp or any of my coworkers, they would have been duty bound to report me to Internal Affairs for investigation due to a policy violation—removal of official police files without proper authorization and disobeying a direct order from the chief of police. It may have resulted in a suspension or termination as the consequences of my deliberate indiscretion. So why did I put my career at risk?

I recognized this investigation was unique. I understood that this type of investigation with this particular cast of characters, to the best of my knowledge, had never been done before, and no one in his right mind would believe me if I told the story. The investigative file with its Klan memorabilia, many of which are exhibited in the photo insert, was the sole physical evidence of the significance of my unique, innovative endeavor, and I wanted a record of it other than word-of-mouth recollections that erode with time and, in the case of my cop peers, alcohol.

The active phase of my Ku Klux Klan investigation was "officially" over. I was proud of my department and myself as a black American, that during this entire investigation no cross was ever burned in the city limits nor in the unincorporated areas of Colorado Springs. "Ron Stallworth—Klansman" disappeared from the scene, never to be heard from again by any of the Colorado Springs chapter membership. My calls to David Duke ceased as well. My investigation of the Ku Klux Klan was concluded.

As for that ringing phone the night I was packing up the files? That very evening, Bell's Nightingale, the black-owned nightclub that had hosted Stokely Carmichael during my first undercover assignment back in 1975, was holding a fund-raiser on behalf of David Scott Lee, the fifteen-year-old black murderer who killed an innocent white man. Later that evening, a cross was burned outside of the nightclub. Were those calls attempts by Ken to tell me about the cross-burning plans for the night? I will never know.

No responsibility was ever acknowledged for the cross burning.

AFTERWORD

Following the official end of the investigation in April 1979 I continued receiving intelligence reports regarding KKK activity. Some of it was legitimate and I followed up on it to the extent that I could, always concerned about my name being recognized as a "Klansman" and aware that I had been ordered by my chief to "disappear." Other information that came my way was from Officer Ed types seeking to get recognized as consequential contributors to the investigation and thus be worthy of consideration for transfer to the Intelligence Unit. In this vein, the most egregious was still Officer Ed. Some of the information he forwarded to me was so obviously inconsequential that I refused to accept it for inclusion in the new file that I generated in the absence of my original investigation. His efforts to ingrain himself in the investigation and curry favor with Sergeant Trapp were never realized during the remainder of my employment with the CSPD. I never received any further information regarding Klan cross burnings or heard from any of the PLP members or representatives of the alphabet soup anti-Klan protest groups in Colorado Springs.

My role as an undercover narcotics investigator continued even after the KKK investigation was concluded. Lieutenant Arthur received a promotion to captain thus creating another obstacle for me to have to eventually confront. I decided my fate in law enforcement would be better served in another agency, where I didn't have Arthur as an impediment to my career aspirations, so I left.

I spent a year as special assignment to the Colorado Attorney General's Organized Crime Strike Force, but it did not last long. I began seeking newer, greener pastures. After a two year (1980–82) stint in Phoenix working as an investigator with the Arizona Drug Control District/Arizona Criminal Intelligence Systems Agency, I landed an undercover narcotics investigator job with the Wyoming Attorney General's Division of Criminal Investigation. Within four years (1982–86) of being the sole black cop in Wyoming's sea of white population I was recruited and eventually hired as a narcotics investigator with the Utah Department of Public Safety's Narcotics & Liquor Law Enforcement Bureau. It was in Utah that I achieved a significant milestone in my law enforcement career.

There was an influx of crack cocaine from Los Angeles being dealt by Crip and Blood gang members in Salt Lake City. I researched and authored a report outlining a strategic response to their presence. That report led to the creation of the Salt Lake Area Gang Project (Metro Gang Unit), the first multi-jurisdictional gang suppression and diversion unit in the state. My report spawned the eventual creation of several similar anti-gang efforts in Utah. The Salt Lake Area Gang Project is currently in its twenty-seventh year of operation.

In the early 1990s I also researched and wrote several reports, books, and magazine articles on the correlation between so-called gangster rap music and street gang culture. I became a nationally recognized lecturer on the subject—testifying before Congress on three occasions—and was acclaimed by my peers as the "foremost law enforcement authority on the subject."

Considering I sought a law enforcement career for the purpose of becoming a high school P.E. teacher, I achieved a level of success that I could never have imagined when I interviewed for the police cadet job as a nineteen year old back in 1972. Over the years I received an official commendation from the CSPD and Organized Crime Strike Force in recognition for my undercover work. The Drug Enforcement Administration and Bureau of Alcohol, Tobacco, Firearms and Explosives gave me certificates of commendation for my work in educating their special agents on the intricacies of street gang culture. The National Gang Crime Research Center presented me with their Frederic Milton Thrasher Outstanding National Leadership Lifetime Achievement Award in recognition of my work identifying the correlation between gangster rap music and street gang culture. In addition, the Utah Department of Public Safety twice presented me with their Distinguished Service Award. I now live with my wife in El Paso, Texas.

Chuck, my white alter ego, continued on a distinguished career path with the CSPD, eventually retiring as a sergeant. Jimmy Rose, on the other hand, took a divergent career path in law enforcement. Within about three years after my departure from the department, Jimmy, too, made the decision to leave and expand his investigative potential. He joined the Drug Enforcement Administration as a special agent where he later became a supervisor. He eventually retired and now lives abroad.

As for Chuck Howarth, the leader of the Posse Comitatus, he followed a colorful path after the end of my investigation and departure from the police department. In May 1982, two years after I left the department, I learned of a multi-agency investigation involving the CSPD which resulted in the arrest of ten people for allegedly selling dynamite, blasting caps, time fuses, detonating cords, and automatic weapons. Among those arrested was Chuck Howarth. When a search warrant was executed at his business, investigators found KKK robes and literature.

A Denver Police spokesperson told a newspaper reporter that Howarth was the apparent leader of the United Klans of America and, by his own admission, he held the title of Exalted Cyclops. Had my investigation been allowed to continues could we possibly have anticipated this development and stopped Howarth in his tracks? Unfortunately we will never know the answer. He was eventually sentenced to two years in prison for illegal possession of explosives and incendiary devices. He has since passed away.

The CSPD indeed made great progress from that November day in 1972 when I was asked whether I could be like Jackie Robinson and not fight back against whites in the department who might disparage and belittle me. It is a much better department since diversity was embraced in its ranks. I am proud to say that I once wore the uniform and badge of the Colorado Springs Police Department.

Following the events of the investigation, the CSPD continued to evolve in its acceptance of blacks within its ranks. Within about three months of my hiring as a police cadet, a black I.D. technician was hired, followed by four black officers a couple of months later. One of these, Robert Sapp, became the first black sergeant in the department's history. Approximately one year after becoming a cadet, the department hired its first black female cadet. She later joined the ranks of police officers but was not the first female to achieve this position.

In incremental numbers, blacks were added to the CSPD officer rolls during the remainder of my employment. One of these, Fletcher Howard, was promoted to commander in 2008, the third highest rank in the department. He retired in 2016 after thirty-eight years of service. A March 28, 2016 *Gazette* article on minority hiring in the CSPD, cited the following statistics on black police officer employment:

1—Lieutenant (female)
4—Sergeants
25—Officers

No more need to be Jackie Robinson.

Today, I am often asked by those familiar with my story if there are any parallels to our current times and my undercover investigation forty years ago? My answer is always the same, a resounding and unequivocal yes!

The hate-fueled, bigoted rhetoric and terroristic intent of white supremacist thinkers like David Duke, Fred Wilkens, and Ken O'Dell was in keeping with the long generational arc of the Ku Klux Klan dating back to its founding immediately after the Civil War. We see and hear echoes of that same rhetoric and intent in the political climate of today. In August of 2017, in Charlottesville, Virginia, white nationalists gathered for the Unite the Right rally. David Duke was in attendance, and a protester was murdered when an alt-right white supremacist drove into a crowd. A tragedy, and the direct parallel to my own experiences with the Klan and David Duke in the 1970s is pretty clear.

Ken O'Dell once mentioned to me that the Klan was going to set up their own border patrol to watch for "wetbacks" coming across the Rio Grande border to El Paso, Texas. He said the Klan would be armed with scope rifles and they would try to shoot the wetbacks to prevent them from entering the United States. Couple O'Dell's words with Klan Grand Wizard David Duke's 1977 statement in the Klan newspaper *The Crusader,* "We believe very strongly white people are becoming second-class citizens in this country . . . When I think of America, I think of a white country." Duke went on to elaborate that one thousand Klansmen would patrol the back roads and midnight border crossings of "illegal immigrants" coming from Mexico into the United States along the San Ysidro, California, border. These sentiments and ideas run parallel to Donald Trump's presidential campaign mantra of building ". . . a great wall the length of the Mexican border to keep out their rapists and drug dealers."

The white nationalist, nativist politics that we see today were first imagined and applied by David Duke during the heyday of his Grand Wizardship, and the time of my undercover Klan investigation. This hatred has never gone away, but has been reinvigorated in the dark corners of the internet, Twitter trolls, alt-right publications, and a nativist president in Trump.

Though the Republican Party of the nineteenth century, being the party of Lincoln, was the opposition to the rise of the Ku Klux Klan and white supremacist domination insofar as America's newly freed Black slaves were concerned; it is my belief that the Republican Party of the twenty-first century finds a symbiotic connection to white nationalist groups like the Klan, neo-Nazis, skinheads, militias, and alt-right white supremacist thinking. Evidence of this began in the Lyndon Johnson administration with the departure of Southern Democrats (Dixiecrats) to the Republican Party in protest of his civil rights agenda. The Republicans began a spiral slide to the far right that embraced all things abhorrent to nonwhites.

David Duke twice ran for public office in Louisiana as a Democrat and lost. When he switched his affiliation to Republican, because he was closer in ideology and racial thinking to the GOP than to the Democrats, and ran again for the Louisiana House of Representatives, the conservative voters in his district rewarded him with a victory. In each case his position on the issues remained the same; white supremacist/ethno-nationalist endorsement of a race-centered rhetoric and nativist populism. What changed were the voters. Democrats rejected Duke's politics while Republicans embraced him.

As for the Progressive Labor Party's (PLP) protest efforts against Duke and the Ku Klux Klan, that thread, too, is historically connected to the modern-day protest efforts of the so-called Antifa, anti-facists, radical communists, socialists, and anarchists. The PLP, like the Antifa, were dedicated to fighting far right extremism. Like the Antifa movement the PLP rejected the police and government authority to keep far right extremism in check. The two believe government, particularly the police, aid and abet far right extremist like the Ku Klux Klan and cannot be trusted to act in the best interest of the public because they follow the rules as established in the U.S. Constitution. To that end both the PLP and Antifa believe aggressive and, if necessary, physical confrontation is appropriate with no regard for consequences. Our history is always in our present.

I know that in spite of my varied career accomplishments, the one that will always most excite and intrigue is the KKK investigation and how I was able to con the Grand Wizard, David Duke, and his coterie of followers. It has defined me in ways unimaginable and has always fascinated those who hear its tale.

ACKNOWLEDGMENTS

To Mr. Elroy Bode, my sophomore English teacher at Austin High School in El Paso, Texas (1969). An award-winning published author, Mr. Bode graciously agreed to "take me back to class" and edit my manuscript.

My relationship with Mr. Bode came full circle when I moved back to El Paso in 2016 after a forty-four-year absence. He was my teacher, became my friend, and then assumed the mantle of mentor. Talks with him were deeply cherished. I always felt like I was back in school, soaking up the wisdom of his years, especially anything pertaining to the art of writing (he was the one who instilled in me that I had a creative talent with words). I came away from those cherished moments with a warm glow in my heart and deep thoughts to ponder. My soul was always enriched because of the honor and privilege I had in sharing a brief episode of life with him.

Mr. Bode, sadly, passed away on September 10, 2017. Thank you, Mr. Bode (and to his widow, Phoebe), for allowing me to share those "special" moments with you. Thank you for your kindness, your time, and your patience with me. You were and will always be my "Teacher."

To my wife, Patsy Terrazas-Stallworth, a very loving thank-you. Following the 2004 loss of my first wife to cancer I went through a six year period of wandering in an emotional wilderness. On December 10, 2010 Patsy reentered my life.

Patsy and I graduated from the same high school in 1971 and we both had Mr. Bode for sophomore English, though in different classes. Another common experience we shared was her first husband, too, had passed away from cancer a few months earlier. She lived in El Paso and I lived in Utah and we talked on the phone for over three hours that December day. We spoke every day thereafter, sometimes five hours at a time, at least twice a day, until our May 26, 2017 wedding. Hers were the first eyes to read my manuscript, often offering personal comments which I frequently acted on. She has been my steady rock, my biggest advocate, and, as always, my "Sweet Girl."

To my business manager, Andy Francis, a very special shout-out. None of this would have been possible without your belief in and support of me.

Thanks to Joel Gotler and Murray Weiss with Intellectual Property Group, my literary agency.

To James Melia, my editor at Flatiron Books. It has been my pleasure to work with you on this project. Thank you for your patience with me.

Special thanks to Pete Bollinger for believing in my story from the first time he heard it and feeling it deserved a wider audience.

I am forever grateful to Shaun Redick, Sean McCittrick, and Ray Mansfield of QC Entertainment for believing my story was worthy of being brought to the big screen and set that effort in motion.

Last, but certainly not least, thanks to Jordan Peele and Spike Lee who learned of my story and chose to take it on as a creative project. I am forever in your debt.

In the writing of this book I drew upon my own memory and experiences to recount my investigation into the Klan, and my experiences as a young detective in Colorado Springs. I was also aided in the research and in the writing by other books that I'd like to acknowledge here: *The Autobiography of Malcolm X* by Malcom X as told to Alex Haley; *Criminal Justice in Action* by Larry Gaines and Roger LeRoy Miller; The Southern Poverty Law Center's *Ku Klux Klan: A History of Racism and Violence*; *Days of Rage* by Bryan Burrough; and *Hooded Empire: The Ku Klux Klan in Colorado* by Robert Alan Goldberg.